When JOLSON Was KING

by Richard Grudens

Foreword by
Frankie Laine

When JOLSON Was KING

By
Richard Grudens

Books By Richard Grudens:

The Best Damn Trumpet Player
The Song Stars
The Music Men
Jukebox Saturday Night
Snootie Little Cutie - The Connie Haines Story
Jerry Vale - *A Singer's Life*
The Spirit of Bob Hope
Magic Moments - The Sally Bennett Story
Bing Crosby - Crooner of the Century
Chattanooga Choo Choo - *The Life and Times of the World Famous Glenn Miller Orchestra*
The Italian Crooners Bedside Companion

CELEBRITY PROFILES PUBLISHING

Box 344 Main Street
Stonybrook, New York 11790-0344
(631) 862-8555
celebpro4@aol.com
www.richardgrudens.com

Published by:

Celebrity Profiles Publishing Company

Div. Edison & Kellogg
Box 344 Main Street
Stonybrook, New York 11790-0344
(631) 862-8555 Phone
(631) 862-0139 Fax
Email: celebpro4@aol.com
Website: www.richardgrudens.com

Book Design and Editing by Madeline Grudens

Library of Congress Control Number In Progress

ISBN: 0-9763877-2-7

Printed in the United States of America
King Printing Company Inc.
Lowell, MA 01852

WHEN JOLSON WAS KING

Memories of the World's Greatest Entertainer

TABLE OF CONTENTS

PART ONE

Early Asa

PART TWO

Hard At Work - Going From Rags To Riches

PART THREE

Wives Tales:

PART FOUR - Tributes From Friends
Personal Glimpses In Their Own Words
From The Present

From The Past

PART FIVE

The Songwriters And Their Songs

PART SIX

The Silents Meet The Talkies

PART SEVEN

The Theaters

PART EIGHT

The Jolson Tribute Artists

Foreword

Words From Frankie Laine

A LONG TIME AGO, a fellow by the name of Asa Yoelson took New York's Broadway by storm with his courageous style of singing on the great stage, namely the Winter Garden. The son of a

cantor in Washington, D.C., Asa, now known to everyone as Al Jolson, performed the great music of his time, notably songs like "Mammy," "Swanee," and "Sonny Boy," "California Here I Come," "April Showers," and belting them out from a runway stage, built deep into the orchestra seats, with verve and much

A Young Frankie Laine with Jolson on the set of *Jolson Sings Again*

heart, always telling his adoring audience that " I wanna see your faces," and, "You ain't heard nothin' yet!"

That was my distinct hero, the one person who set the stage for my fledgling career. A dominating, powerful voiced performer who sang out loudly mainly because there was no microphone to help him project his songs.

He often remained after his show's final act and continued to wow his audience until after midnight. No one else did that.
Then along came followers Crosby, Como, Sinatra, Bennett, and Frankie Laine, that's me, and all of us emulated the great Jolson. He

was our hero, our heroic predecessor.

I once met up with Al Jolson on the set of *The Jolson Story* and told him of my reverence for his music, and recently sent Richard Grudens the one photograph taken with Jolson, that I cherish, to place in this book.

Now, I say to you, read about this great man, often called the greatest entertainer of the 20th century. Richard Grudens unveils the sights and sounds of the era and includes Jolson's counterparts, supporters, detractors, musicians, producers, song writers, and includes interesting vignettes of the legendary Shubert Brothers and all of Broadway's other characters.

A colorful and rich biography of the music, the sights and sounds of the early part of the 20th century, of the great Al Jolson.

Frankie Laine

August 2005, SanDiego, CA

Poignant Words

From President
Ronald Reagan

"Al Jolson's accomplishments on the stage, screen and radio are still widely admired and remembered. From The Jazz Singer to The Jolson Story, he delighted countless people, and we are especially proud of his appearances before United States troops during three wars. Quite simply, he was a great showman and a concerned and generous citizen."

President Ronald Reagan, May 25, 1985

A letter Read by comedian Joey Adams on Al Jolson Day in New York City in the Roosevelt Hotel on May 25, 1985 and later presented to Albert Jolson, Jr.

Introduction

You may ask what's the relevance of Jolson today? Well, it's like asking: what's the relevance of the Wright Brothers or Thomas Edison? Like them he started it all---everything that we take for granted today.

Some time ago I had decided to embark upon a search about the life and career of Al Jolson, he being someone who has haunted me before, and ever since my first writings and interviews of many of his successors, both singers and musicians, and in all cases, entertainers. His name cropped up regularly and from every direction. It followed me everywhere in my quest to learn about Crosby, Sinatra, Como, Laine, and others who claim him as mentor. He is the rock they built their careers upon. The first superstar. The first crooner, and for certain, the first popular singer. And he didn't need a microphone.

What was going on during the King's reign? Who were the players? Who helped him? Who kept him down? Whom did he help? Whom did he love, besides himself? Who employed him? Who loved him?

Who best benefited from his reign as the King of Show Business? How did he endear himself to so many?

Like many lifetime Jolson followers, my personal introduction to Al Jolson's repertoire of songs occurred in 1946, long after his great success, when Columbia Pictures produced an autobiographical movie entitled *The Jolson Story*. In this terrific and entertaining film, filled with Jolson's greatest songs sung with a more mature voice, Larry Parks, a young, tall and handsome actor with shocks of wavy hair, lip-synched Jolson's timeless evergreens while Jolson actually sang them off-camera. The vitality of the mature Jolson voice matched well with Parks' bearing and physical simulation. It was so convincing that, when I later saw photos of the actual Jolson, I couldn't believe that, although short and diminutive in stature like many performers of his day, he was a perfect show-business specimen and suited to his bearing, and Larry Parks was the best match that could be found to represent him.

By 1946, Jolson was well beyond middle age, although we are not yet sure of the exact date of his birth.

At fourteen years old, a member of the Owl Patrol of the Boy Scouts of America, and smitten by Jolson's greatness, I applied blackface while my brother, Bob, worked a portable phonograph playing the movie's tracks behind a curtain. I reflected on one knee - and emulated a few Jolson tunes, including "My Mammy" during Parents Night in the basement meeting room of our local church in Brooklyn, New York. That's how affected I was by Jolson. To me he was sensational.

Parks' brilliant portrayal of Jolson paved the way for an unexpected Columbia Pictures blockbuster and a renewal of Jolson's tumultuous career as the greatest entertainer America has ever known. Al Jolson became a totally reincarnated super entertainer upon the big screen mirrored through Larry Parks. His recordings once again sold in the millions. An entirely new generation had discovered old Jolson classics previously communicated live to his audience 30 years before from elevated proscenium stages of the world's majestic theaters, music halls and palaces, where he had to shout out his songs over the heads of orchestra pit musicians to an anticipating crowd, until he discovered the use of a runway.

Jolson's countenance was eternally eager, his need for an audience's admiration of him almost desperate. He broke the barrier, developing personal intimacy between audience and performer for the first time as he vigorously strode those runways that extended deep through the center of the theater. Bent down on one knee, crooning his classics to a mesmerized crowd, all he ever wanted was to see into their faces to certify that they idolized him. *The Jolson Story* sharply elevated my interest in all singers and their songs that has translated into a career of writing about singers and musicians from that day through today.

Playing earlier Jolson recordings led me to realize that

Jolson's mature voice, as recorded for *The Jolson Story,* was clearly superior to earlier recordings that were tinny, although I must admit that I enjoy them just as much. Due to improved technical recording equipment and some other reasons, Jolson was at his best voice in 1946.

This book is not an adoration, nor is it an expose or psychological study or probe or attempt at special or unique insight to his psyche, or failed marriages or other negative segments of his life. This is a celebration and a guided tour of one man's career that includes coverage of those who lived and interacted with him as well as vignettes about friends and counterparts.

Surfing, as they say today, Al Jolson's wondrous years is what this book is all about.

Celebrate the time and story When Jolson Was King.

Richard Grudens
Stonybrook, New York
October 30, 2005

Bing Crosby Tribute

with Kathryn Crosby

Bing's consummate hero was Al Jolson. Thus he was immensely influenced by Jolson, whose songs he heard over and over on the family's cylinder phonograph and later on the revolutionary 78 shellac discs. The jazzy, exciting music of Jolson and others of the emerging times moved young Crosby along, emotionally arousing his interest and commitment to the craft of singing in a joyous manner.

Bing Crosby

Bing's mother and father had performed regularly in local amateur Gilbert & Sullivan operettas and always brought home the latest recordings for Bing to hear.

"Hey, Mom," Bing said after catching a moment of his mother's obvious enjoyment while listening to and humming the music of "The Merry Widow Waltz." "You really love the music, don't you?" Bing examined the shellac disc closely, wondering how the infinite number of tiny grooves circling round and round could effectively recreate such beautiful sounds through such a tiny needle.

"My renewed interest in singing, and especially in wanting

to perform on a public stage, was mounting day by day. I wound up working in a theatrical prop department whenever traveling shows arrived in town. When Al Jolson's show *Sinbad* came through, as had many shows featuring Willie Howard, Eddie Cantor, Fanny Brice, and Gallagher & Shean, I worked my way to become a theater errand boy and did that several times when Jolson appeared. After listening so often to Al's recordings, it was strangely thrilling to actually see and hear him sing right in front of you. You know what they say: 'You had to be there.' I found that to be quite true."

Bing Crosby, Al Rinker and Harry Barris - The Rhythm Boys

In his 1953 autobiography *Call Me Lucky* Bing said: "You could never forget Al Jolson. He was absolutely electric. When he stepped onto the stage and started to sing, young and old were immediately captured by him. He was irresistible. Nobody in those days did what he did. The audience just elevated immediately. Within the first eight bars he had them in the palm of his hand."

For a while, Bing thought of emulating his hero, but decided that black face singing was not what he pictured for himself.

Bing Crosby:

"Years later, when I got to know Al, he didn't remember me, the lop-eared lad who watched his every move, but I remembered him vividly."

Later, when Bing invited Al to guest on his radio shows, the two would banter:

Bing: "Al, you are indefatigable. If I'd let you, you'd sing all night."

Al: You're no slouch, Bing. Never seen you nappin' over a song, you dog!

Some people say that Bing sought Jolson for his radio appearances because he felt sorry for him during Jolson's absence from the stage

Kathryn Crosby, 2003 - *Madeline Grudens Photo*

and films. Bing denied it, heralding Jolson's greatness being an asset to his shows, and how proud he was to feature his mentor, and was thrilled to be able to perform with him, a dream come true for Bing.

Would there have been a Bing Crosby without an earlier Al Jolson? Jolson was really the first pop singer, wasn't he? Did he pave the road for Crosby's successful journey? Scholars of the genre say yes! Bing, himself, said Yes!. I absolutely agree.

In my conversation one day with Bing's wife, Kathryn Crosby, she emphasized and confirmed the fact. "Their music lives, Richard. Their films live! The gentle humor Bing displayed is a touching, living, wondrous thing. His eyes will never dim and his beauty will never diminish, as will Al Jolson's own legacy survive and transcend time. They were both great performers and loved by so many. "And how I miss Bing. And what I'd give to hear him salute the sunrise with "Cielito Lindo" just one more time."

"I've never seen anyone as relaxed as this kid, Crosby. Scripts mean nothing to him. He drops ad libs any time one occurs to him. On the program we did with Irving Berlin, I figured I'd drop one in on him. So when Bing asked casually: 'Well, what'll we do?' I said, 'You hit the first note and I'll ride along.' So he looked at me, a little surprised, and hit the first note, and I stopped him.

"I said, 'wait a minute, lad. We ain't gonna get any place with a note like that.' You know what the guy shot back at me? He says, nice and easy-like: 'Take that note down to my bank and they'll discount it.' Yes sir, he's a real solid performer, that Crosby, and smart as a whip."

Fortunately for us, in this year of 2006, Bing's friend and record producer Ken Barnes has released a new album "Bing Crosby Meets Al Jolson - The Complete Radio Duets." Barnes and restoration wizard Peter J. Reynolds have rescued the essential Crosby/ Jolson radio performances, restoring the sound quality to a high level in its ninety-nine tracks, featuring every Crosby-Jolson radio duet.

A Probable Interview With Al Jolson

Selling Songs and Jokes

Had I the opportunity to interview Al Jolson while in his prime, here are the questions I would have asked and the probable replies:

Al Jolson and Richard Grudens - *With Some Computer Assistance*

RG: As the complete showman, do you consider yourself a comedian and a singer or just a singer?

AJ: Neither. I consider myself a salesman of both songs and jokes. Just as any other man sells merchandise, I have to sell my goods to the audience.

RG: Yes, but are you selling songs or jokes, or both?

AJ: Both! Even when people say I know how to put a song across, they are merely saying that, like a salesman of shoes or shirts, I know how to sell my goods. That includes my songs and my jokes.

RG: Where did you learn to sell your goods, as you put it?

AJ: I learned the tricks of my trade in small stores. These stores were called vaudevilles, and in these places I picked up many a valuable selling points.

RG: How long have you been involved in this sales training?

AJ: About eighteen years, and I am constantly learning new ways.

RG: For instance?

AJ: Well, I worked in one of the biggest department stores, in my line that means the Winter Garden. When I came to the Winter Garden, I at once saw my greatest opportunity: A long, narrow runway extended from the front of the stage out over the orchestra chairs to the very back row. It was supposed to be used only by the chorus girls as they paraded up and down it. But the moment I saw it I knew it gave me my big chance.

RG: In what way did it help sell your products - singing and joke-telling?

AJ: I used it to get confidential with the audience by running up and down on this platform, stopping for a chat with the people, and by kidding the audience, and the performers in general. And the effect of this method of entertaining or of selling my goods was, and is to this day, truly remarkable.

RG: How did the audience react to this method of you delivering those goods?

AJ: The psychology of the trick is simple. It's a well-known fact that the nearer the average theatergoer can get to the intimate side of stage life, the better pleased he is. The desire for intimacy with stage folk is well known. They want to be a part of the act or interact with stage folk, if possible. Bringing the stage nearer to the people is what the people want - why they come in the first place. It flatters the audience to be close to the performers, especially if they are singled out - extending that personal touch as though you are performing for them alone. That's how it works. If you analyze it, you will see that it is all salesmanship

RG: Thank you Mr. Al Jolson.

Jolsoniana

You Ain't Heard, Or Seen, Nothin' Yet!

JOLSON commanded the Broadway stage for thirty years.

JOLSON was the first singer ever to sell a million records of a single hit. "Sonny Boy."

JOLSON was the first Broadway star to take his show on the road.

JOLSON was the first entertainer to earn $10,000 week before the first World War.

JOLSON'S singing voice was the first to be heard in a full-length motion picture.

JOLSON was the first entertainer to perform for our fighting forces overseas during World War II and again in Korea

JOLSON was the first entertainer to stop a Broadway show and ad lib to the audience.

JOLSON had two biographical films produced covering his fantastic career.

JOLSON had the most successful comeback in show business history.

JOLSON'S Decca album of *The Jolson Story* sold 1,000,000 copies becoming the biggest selling album of all time when it was issued.

JOLSON'S recording of "The Anniversary Song" single was # 1 on England's Hit Parade.

JOLSON earned $3,500,000 from his share of *The Jolson Story*, a record amount for the time.

JOLSON'S patter recording with Bing Crosby of Irving Berlin's "Alexander's Ragtime Band" sold 300,000 copies in one week following a performance on a radio broadcast.

JOLSON still retains the presence and focus of an International Society of about 1000 members 56 years after his passing.

Broadway shows: From JOLSON'S first, *La Belle Paree* through his final Broadway appearance in *Hold On to Your Hats*, he appeared in ten major musical comedies and twenty-nine total productions.

Radio shows: JOLSON was the first star of the *Kraft Music Hall* series, with six radio series in all, beginning in1932 and ending in 1949. The six series comprised 289 broadcasts and 76 guest appearances.

Motion Pictures: Not including the earlier 1923 D.W. Griffith production *Black Magic*, that preceded *The Jazz Singer*, JOLSON appeared in 18 Jolson films, up to and including *Swanee River*, then was reduced to more minor roles in additional films, and, of course, the object of the biographical *Jolson Story* and *Jolson Sings Again* that featured only his voice, except for a short dance scene on the runway in *The Jolson Story*.

Here is the list of films and date of release:

THE HONEYMOON EXPRESS 2/13/13 SILENT

UNTITLED 5/11/18 (Produced to benefit for the Police Benevolent Association, but never shown commercially).

AL JOLSON IN A PLANTATION ACT 10/17/26 (HIS FIRST TALKING PICTURE)

THE JAZZ SINGER 10/6/27

THE SINGING FOOL 9/19/28

SAY IT WITH SONGS 8/6/29

MAMMY 3/26/30

BIG BOY 9/11/30

HALLELUJAH, I'M A BUM 2/8/33

WONDER BAR 2/28/34

GO INTO YOUR DANCE 5/2/35

THE SINGING KID 4/3/36

ROSE OF WASHINGTON SQUARE 5/5/39

HOLLYWOOD CAVALCADE 10/13/39

SWANEE RIVER 12/29/39

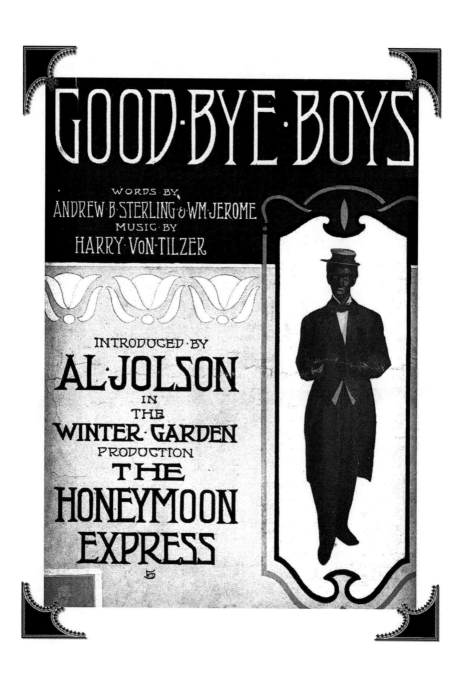

RHAPSODY IN BLUE 6/27/45

THE JOLSON STORY 10/10/46

Records: JOLSON made 205 original, commercially available recordings in the studio, not including 26 unissued or rejected, and not including reformulated albums and reissues. First recording documented in 1910 with Edison Records backed by the Edison Orchestra in New York City. His last recording made in Los Angeles on July 17, 1950, with Gordon Jenkins Orchestra and Chorus, composed of four Stephen Foster song selections for Decca records.

Jolson has more recordings converted to CDs than any other performer.

The NBC Questionnaire

This standard new star Questionnaire was submitted to Al Jolson when he signed with the National Broadcasting Company in 1935. Jolson filled in the answers, but not in the manner NBC wanted. The object was information for press releases.

NAME: Al Jolson

NICKNAME: No answer

REAL NAME: Asa Joelson

MANAGER, IF ANY: The wife

PHONE: Don't try anything.

PERSONAL PRESS AGENT: Mahatma Ghandi

TALENT (Specially on Radio): Get paid every week.

HEIGHT: 5-10 **WEIGHT**: 160

COMPLEXION: Dark HAIR: Brown

WHERE AND WHEN BORN: In bed at night.

PARENTS: (Did their learning's or characteristics have any bearing on your radio success? Were they talented?): Rev. Morris Yoelson, formerly a Cantor, if that means anything.

ANY OTHER MEMBERS OF YOUR FAMILY MUSICALLY OR DRAMATICALLY INCLINED?: Yes, musically. Brother is Harry Jolson, the vaudevillian.

MARITAL STATUS (wife): Ruby Keeler Jolson, status quo.

CHILDREN: None

RADIO HISTORY, first audition: October 1932

FIRST PROFESSIONAL ENGAGEMENT (Any special circumstances, anecdotes, humorous incidents): Nice weather we're having.

CHRONOLOGICAL HISTORY (EXPERIENCE ON THE AIR INCLUDING ANY PRIOR TO NBC WITH DATES, COMMENTS, ETC.): None and none and none.

PROFESSIONAL BACKGROUND (Previous stage, opera, concert, and other experience): La Scala Opera Company, Jitney Opera Company; Heckscher Opera Company; Heckscher Theater, New York; Minsky's Burlesque; Buenos Aires Opera Company; South America; Metropolitan Opera Company.

EDUCATIONAL BACKGROUND (Schools, colleges, dramatic and musical training, name of instruments and teachers): Yale, Harvard, Princeton, Vassar, Ossining (Twice)

WHAT WERE YOUR SCHOOL AND COLLEGE ACTIVITIES (i.e. sports, singing, debating): Catching butterflies.

COLLEGE DEGREE: 3rd degree Fahrenheit

FRATERNITIES: B'nai B'rith - they were also sore at me.

LODGES OR CLUBS: Ancient Order of Hog Callers, Ancient Order Hibernians, Knights of Columbus, Knights of the Road, Knights of Gladness.

DO YOU LIVE IN THE CITY OR COUNTRY AND WHY: That's what I want to know.

WHAT DO YOU DO TO AMUSE YOURSELF: See school and college activities and Who's Who in Hackensack, Groves Dictionary,

Henderson's Seed Catalog, and the World Almanac.

WHEN AND WHERE DO YOUR WRITE, SING, PRACTICE, OR REHEARSE? (State hours and circumstances) : Pay toilet at the Astor.

HAVE YOU ANY SUGGESTIONS AS TO PRESS STORIES REGARDING YOURSELF?: Take the aircaster, Ben Gross, and those of that type and throw in Louis Reid. Oh, hell, throw them all in.

Jolson did not fill in the remaining 250 questions on the Questionnaire.

Never A Racist - Always A Performer

"Criticizing Jolson about blackface is absurd. You can't criticize one period of history using the standards of another period." Steve Allen, 1999.

Since the passing of Al Jolson in 1950, questions of his past blackface performances have surfaced. Al Jolson achieved immense fame on Broadway placing his white-gloved hands over his heart, his face covered with burnt cork, bent down on one knee, pleading:

> George Burns: "Working in 'black,' covering your skin with burnt cork and painting on wide white lips, was an important part of vaudeville. It had no racial meaning at all, even great black stars like Bert Williams put on blackface. Performers wearing black didn't imitate blacks, most of them spoke in their ordinary voices. The only thing blackface meant was the person wearing it was working in show business."

"Mammy! Mammy! I'm comin' I'm comin! Sorry that I made you wait," his voice carrying up to the rafters to the delight of an adoring audience.

Understandably, that style of performance would not be acceptable to today's audiences, except perhaps in England or Australia where there is more indifference to such acts.

The tradition of blackface in show business was well established when Jolson was in his prime. In 1904, after trying vainly to become a vaudeville comedian, Jolson tried the blackface routine in desperation at the suggestion of a fellow blackfaced

MY MAMMY

THE SUN SHINES EAST — THE SUN SHINES WEST

As Sung By
AL JOLSON
In Sinbad

Words by
JOE YOUNG
and
SAM LEWIS

Music by
WALTER DONALDSON

Irving Berlin Inc.

monologist.

"Wearing blackface is like a mask," he said to Jolson, "You will look and feel more like a performer.

The advice, well taken, turned him into a powerful and much-loved performer when he applied the burnt cork to his face and performed his magic. To Jolson, it was the equivalent of wearing a period costume. The character he was portraying in concert with his brother Harry and partner Joe Palmer in the act Jolson, Palmer, and Jolson, became energized with this new look, prompting fresh enthusiasm from audiences. Earlier, his counterpart, entertainer Eddie Cantor and other major stars of the era had also donned blackface as part of their act, but only on vaudeville stages.

Al Jolson decided blackface would enhance his theatrical qualities. There was never a thought in his mind that this would degrade blacks. There were scores of minstrel shows performing everywhere at that time. Even black performers themselves applied burnt cork to darken their faces, and for the same, honest reasons. While with the famed Lew Dockstader's Minstrels, Jolson performed in about 100 theaters from Maine to Virginia in 1908 and in twenty-six cities in 1909 from Niagara Falls, New York to Kansas City, Missouri, as a blackfaced comedian and singer. Dockstader's troupe was highly respected and was always booked into the premier theaters and opera houses.

Jolson was never a racist in any sense of the word. He never

Michael Rogin, Political Science professor-University of California at Berkeley, 1999. "Jolson is incomprehensible and inconceivable without blackface. That's what he did. He is part of American nostalgia, but you can't just sanitize him and get rid of the embarrassing parts. That's a shocking falsification of history."

displayed signs of ethnic hatred. Once, he learned that ragtime musician Eubie Blake and songwriter Noble Sissle, relatively unknowns at the time, were refused service in a restaurant because they were black. Jolson had read about it in the newspaper and telephoned them to "...try to make it up to them" and took them to dinner in a limo, stating: "I'll punch out anyone who'll try to kick us out!" he told his fellow performers. They dined in Jolson's favorite Jewish deli restaurant and later spent the evening together eating pastrami sandwiches and listening to Jolson sing in his big automobile. Jolson often sang Sissle & Blake's evergreen standard "I'm Just Wild About Harry."

Sissle attended Jolson's funeral, as they remained friends. And wasn't it Jolson who crossed the line performing with Cab Calloway in *The Singing Kid*? As a kid in Washington, D.C. Jolson performed in the streets with black friends, and later in life, would haunt black cabarets in Harlem, golf with Joe Louis and shoot craps with Bill "Bojangles" Robinson. And his character "Gus", was no menial character, easily outmatching and outwitting white people in his various roles on stage and in films.

Unfortunately, Jolson's reputation becomes unfairly tarnished by the insensitive past and forbidding present. To many, blackface performances evoke unpleasant memories. At that time white performers blatantly borrowed emerging jazz music from black performers who were held back performing their own in mainstream show business. But that, too, was part of history and you can't sweep history under the rug or alter the atmosphere that existed at the time. You can't reach back and attach blame where acceptance prevailed. If you do, then everyone who bought a ticket is equally as guilty. No, that is unfair and much too heavy baggage to endure. Reaching back to the 1840s through the early years of the 20th century, blackface minstrel shows were the foundation of American entertainment. History will record this period of blackface performances as just what it was, right or wrong, sincere, accepted entertainment of the times.

You may recall that in many Hollywood films Italian Americans and even African Americans appeared as American Indians in Westerns. And, in the film *The Magnificent Seven* the great Eli Wallach appeared as a callous and murderous Mexican Bandit. Eli Wallach is a Jew. In August of 2005, I recounted that scenario to Eli Wallach at a book signing garden party in East Hampton after his performance with his wife, Anne Jackson, at the John Drew Theater. His reply: " You know, all that doesn't matter.

We are just actors. And, did you know that I'm the only living person left from that movie. They are all gone."

Jolson was just an actor in costume. Over the years Jolson impersonators have donned the historical costume which includes blackface and have performed before Jolson followers ever since Jolson passed in 1950, a few years after his comeback via the

Jolson in *The Jazz Singer*

wonderful bio-film *The Jolson Story* and it's sequel *Jolson Sings Again*.

Clive Baldwin, the best known, long-running Jolson impersonator, self-proclaimed as the last minstrel, toured Jolson conventions, performing in blackface, mostly to older fans and dedicated Jolson followers.

"I am the curator of a kind of a museum," Baldwin once said a few years ago, "I am a martyr for my time, and for what I do, I could probably get lynched!"

Baldwin views blackface performing as "an act of brotherly affection toward the black man" and claims that such performers "humanized blacks for white audiences, thereby laying the groundwork for racial equality."

There have been many Jolson impersonators, some good and some not so good. Worldwide there are over 1000 members of the International Al Jolson Society and many more uncounted fans who still enjoy Jolson performances. There also exists myriad impersonators of Bing Crosby, Eddie Cantor, Frank Sinatra, Dean Martin, and Elvis Presley. They don't have to deal with the problem that Jolson impersonators are confronted with in order to emulate their beloved performers of the past. By dressing up the way they do in today's climate of political correctness, Jolson performers face criticism although their intentions are to present a mirrored lovefest of their departed favorite and not to fuel political or racial argument. It's clear to me Jolson celebrated a love for his audience in the best way he knew how, in blackface or otherwise. To me he still retains the title of The World's Greatest Entertainer.

Bombo Review by Gordon Whyte in *Billboard*, Oct. 22, 1921:

"When this writer first saw Al Jolson he was a vaudeville artist. This was shortly after he terminated his career as a minstrel. He is a vaudeville artist today - a peerless one...he has his public, and it supports him in everything he chooses to do."

Forever Al

by Anthony Di Florio III

In 1950, a young girl named Dolores Kaczynski started a fan club for her favorite singer, Al Jolson. She couldn't have known that before the year was over it would become a memorial society upon his death on October 23rd. Dolores would grow up to marry a man named Norb Kontowicz and 55 years later both the marriage and the society are still going strong.

Who would have believed that the most famous entertainer of the first half of the twentieth century would still have an active, truly International Society in his honor at the beginning of the 21st Century! Well, I'm certain that Al Jolson would not have been surprised. Jolie was no slouch in the self-confidence department; but even he would be impressed by the devotion showed him by his

900-member strong International Al Jolson Society.

The IAJS is much more than a fan club. It is a professionally-run organization with a constitution, by-laws and elected officers. The Jolson Society has a yearly convention at locations in the US and the UK. It publishes two excellent journals a year and quarterly newsletters filled with fascinating articles on Jolson, his contemporaries, his times and his legacy.

Despite the fact that his talent may seem dated, or worse, politically incorrect in these times; there is something about the power of his charisma that still attracts fans who can see through the antique vehicles that carry his talent.

Jolson was the biggest star in the world before the Great Depression of the 1930's and the rise of the crooners. All singers who followed him were influenced by him. But he was also influenced by his successors. After the war, thanks to a Technicolor fantasy called *The Jolson Story,* which featured his voice, a new generation of fans was captivated by the now deeper voiced, part-time crooning Jolson. It was the greatest comeback in showbiz history, and Jolson had an incredible five year run that would probably have continued if he hadn't literally worked himself to death entertaining the troops during the Korean War. It is the grateful veterans who have carried the torch for Jolie these many years; passing along their love for his music to their children and grandchildren. Television showings of *The Jolson Story* and its sequel, *Jolson Sings Again* continue to win him new fans; and newer technologies: video tape,

Dolores Kontowicz

CDs, DVDs will probably keep his talent alive well into the 22nd century and beyond.

Early Asa
The Road to Greatness

After considerable effort researching many facts, angles, and frames of reference covering Al Jolson's life and career, and considering the existence of numerous past and current books, as well as a fair number of magazine articles written about, and by him, this abridged window of his life is presented as a fundamentally, but distilled endeavor. It has been certified by a number of Jolson aficionados and scholars, acknowledged within, as a valid biographical sketch:

Emigrating

JOLSON BROS.
Al & HARRY 1899

from Seredzius, Lithuania in 1894, when he was about six (or possibly older), Asa Yoelson (possibly, Joelson), along with his mother and siblings, arrived at Ellis Island, New York, where he was met by Moshe Reuben Yoelson, his father, who had preceded him four years earlier immigrating himself from their native land and established himself as a Cantor in a poor Washington, D.C. synagogue.

Within a year of their arrival his mother Naomi died giving birth. His father remarried within a year, and Asa, devastated at witnessing his mother's passing, distanced himself from his stepmother and sought a life outside the home in a make-believe world of show business. From the time he was just a boy, he never remained at home very much. Besides Asa, to be known as Al, there were siblings: Sisters Rose, Etta and Gertrude, and an older brother by three years, Hirsch, to be known as Harry.

Al With His Father

Young Al and older brother Harry became enamored by performers who worked in local burlesque shows. They would haunt their neighborhood Bijou Theater to attend the popular dramas *Uncle Tom's Cabin* and *Ten Nights in a Barroom*. The two brothers would sing popular songs of the day in front of the Raleigh Hotel and collect the coins thrown at them that they used for admissions to even more area theater presentations. When Zangwill's play, *Children of the Ghetto*, opened in Washington, the show had solicited children for the New York street scenes. Al tried his first stage appearance as one of the children, that is until his father

An Early Asa Selling Newspapers

learned of it and dragged him home. Then he caught the attention of a Fagin-like character who encouraged him to try out his soprano voice in a vaudeville show known as Rich & Hoppe's Big Company of Fun Makers.

After experiencing that limited engagement, nothing could keep the young performer and his brother, Harry, away from metropolitan Washington theaters. He admired the baggy-trousered comedians and vaudeville singers. On several occasions he sang with some of the performers when they would request the audience to join in, which he did, and even when he wasn't invited. Wearied by his father's constant scolding, his sister's nagging, the unwanted, ever-present Hebrew lessons, and a need to perform, both he and his brother ran away to become hopeful vaudeville performers. Al was about thirteen. Harry was sixteen.

Al's father had to bring him back home from these runaway excursions, but, undaunted, Al would run off to join with varied show business endeavors over and over again. His father even whipped him, but he returned to the Bijou hoping to find a way to realize his dream. For certain, his father wanted him to sing in the synagogue as the seventh cantor in an unbroken family line, but all this young man could think of was to someday sing in a theater before a live audience.

When Al was about fifteen, he entertained soldiers and miners in several small Pennsylvania towns, then, when the Walter Main Circus passed through Harrisburg, he joined the troupe where

Harry Jolson: "Today a boy would not get far on such journeys. He would be reported and returned by police in a day. But in those days hundreds, even thousands, of orphanded boys were forced to make their own way, earning a pitiful existance and slept in doorways and barrels, and no one was interested in them unless they committed a crime."

he was able to perform a song or two. His circus life ended at York, Pennsylvania, so he traveled to Baltimore on a train, and became a newsboy, sang in saloons, and was found by local police, who was searching for him, and brought to St. Mary's Industrial School for

Boys, and enrolled him. But that effort too couldn't hold back the future great entertainer.

For months afterwards he repeatedly left home only to be brought back. It is said he sang from the audience during

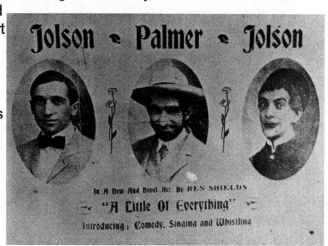

Jolson ❧ Palmer ❧ Jolson

In A New And Novel Act By REN SHIELDS

"A Little Of Everything"

Introducing: Comedy, Singing and Whistling

the vaudeville act of Eddie Leonard, then toured with Al Reeves' Burlesque company. All were minor learning events and frustrating.

October 1900, found him performing with the Victoria Burlesquers featuring headliner Agnes Behler, wherein he acted as her "foil" and sometimes solo singer. The following year, he joined with Fred Moore in an vaudeville act named Master Joelson & Fred Moore. They both then coupled with the Al Reeves Famous Big Company where Al developed much of his future performing style.

A New York Minstrel Theater

The Cast of *La Belle Paree* - 1911 - Winter Garden Theater

Breaking with Moore after a short touring event, Al and Harry got together and formed an act they called *The Hebrew and the Cadet*. They eventually linked with known vaudevillian Joe Palmer, who worked from a wheelchair. The act was named Jolson, Palmer and Jolson, the 'e' being dropped from "Joelson," legend says, because the three names could not jointly fit on either a marquee or a theatrical sign. Harry soon dropped out to perform on his own, and, soon after, Al also began working as a single.

Off to the west coast, Jolson met Henrietta Keller, fell in love with her and married. A neglectful husband dedicated to his more important task of an eventual show business success, their marriage became strained by his absence and indifference to home life.

After appearances with Walter Sanford's Stock Company, Al Jolson joined Lew Dockstader's Minstrels, a respected and celebrated blackface performing troupe. Jolson honed important theatrical skills there and remained for over one year. Within this group Jolson slowly achieved growing measures of prominence, becoming the show's most significant performer.

Now personally managed by Arthur Klein, Jolson broke with Dockstader and began to earn big money, signing with the ubiquitous Shubert Brothers. His Shubert debut was in the show *La Belle Paree* in 1911, performed at the brand-new Winter Garden Theater in New York, owned by the Shubert's. The Winter Garden would become the home of Al Jolson's thriving, crowning Broadway achievements. The success of that show brought even greater success to the production

Tomorrow Night
And All Week
MATS. WED. and SAT.

ENGAGEMENT EXTRAORDI-
NARY
LAST MUSICAL SHOW OF
THE SEASON.

AL JOLSON
in
"ROBINSON CRUSOE JR."

WITH THE ORIGINAL N. Y. WINTER GARDEN
SUMPTUOUS, STUPENDOUS PRODUCTION OF
TEN TREMENDOUS, TUMULTUOUS SCENES,
AND PERSONNEL OF 200, INCLUDING THE
FAR-FAMED BEAUTY BRIGADE.
NIGHTS, 50c TO $2.50. WED. AND SAT. MATS., 50c TO $2.00.

Jolson in *Sinbad*, 1918 - Winter Garden Theater

that followed, *Vera Violetta*, and featured French star Mlle. Gaby Deslys. Here, he seduced his audience and rendered every other performer's act inconsequential.

His star finally aloft, Jolson quickly became a monumental star and the Shubert Brothers' biggest money-maker between 1911 and 1925. Jolson had at last accomplished his long-fought, hard-won goal, becoming a virtual one-man show that dominated all other Broadway contenders. His first recordings with Victor Records were made between 1911 & 1913.

Through 1916, mostly at the Winter Garden, Jolson starred triumphantly in *The Whirl of Society, Honeymoon Express, Dancing Around*, and *Robinson Crusoe, Jr.* Each show was followed with national tours. He was the first entertainer to take a big-time Broadway show on the road. Jolson performed as his sterling character sobriquet "Gus" in blackface, both singing and performing. Many nights found Jolson extending the shows' hour beyond it's normal conclusion by performing great song hits for an adoring audience who could not get enough of his extemporaneous repertoire of patter, jokes, and songs. He was every show's pilot and manager, taking advantage of every comedy opening and dynamic opportunity for a song.

With World War I in progress Jolson became active selling government war bonds and performing for wounded troops in hospitals and army camps, singing all the great songs that had endeared him to everyone.

To the adoring public, the show itself did not matter. It was *Jolson* that did. Jolson, the consummate artist presenting entertainment never heard before. Jolson, a bold, loud, dominating, impressive entertainer with always a perfect presence delivering electrifying performances of songs and comedy to appreciative audiences.

In the show *Sinbad*, his debut delivery of the song "Swanee" made it's author, (Tin Pan Alley songwriter George Gershwin) famous. "Swanee" typified Jolson's great presence with a song. It became Jolson's signature song and will always be identified with him. As this guide into Al Jolson life unfolds, it will reveal the heart of Al Jolson through his contemporaries, his family, the musicians, the songwriters, the show business entrepreneurs who proliferated Broadway, Tin Pan Alley, and radio in pursuit of their own dreams, and words from succeeding show business stars and their reflection on his incumbancy as the World's Greatest Entertainer.

Each protaganist needed the existence of the other. Theater owners required new plays and "angels," to back shows with hard cash. Producers required theaters to showcase their magnificent productions. Musical directors needed composers, lyricists, arrangers, musicians, and performers. Directors needed playwrights, performers, songwriters, costumes, and musicians. The entire panorama of personnel made the show a *show*.

Jolson was the *entire* show.

★ ADMIT ONE ★

LEW DOCKSTADER

AND HIS SEVENTY REAL MINSTRELS

AL. JOLSON
NEIL O'BRIEN

EDDIE MAZIER - WILL OAKLAND
REESE V. PROSSER - W.H. THOMPSON
HERBERT WILLISON - WILL H. HALLET
JOS. NATUS - TOMMY HYDE
MASTER KEEGAN - PETE DENZEL

- AND -

60 MORE "CORKERS"
MINSTRELS

Evenings 25c, 35c, 50c, 75c, $1.00 - Matinee Monday, Wednesday and Saturday, 25c and 50c

Next Sunday Night

Always the Best Show in Town

25c
50c **10 BIG ACTS 10** 25c
50c

TICKETS
All Theatres **HERRICK** COPLEY
SQUARE

Telephone Back Bay 2329 - Back Bay 2330 - Back Bay 2331

Dockstader and the Minstrel Shows

" I am, for tonight, in your very esteemed honor, a harlequin in blackface. Mine is to sing, or to dance, or to read my melodic nonsense, at your will. The audience is king tonight." Al Jolson, 1914.

Tightly crowded on a small stage sits a uniform semi-circle row of blackfaced male entertainers dressed in red and white vertical-striped pants and an oversized white bow-tie, each with a tambourine in his lap held with both hands while singing Stephen Foster's "De Camptown Races." In the back row players feature a bass violin, snare drum, cornets, banjos, spoons, and violins. The name could have been something like Christy's Ethiopian Serenaders, who, as a group, then tap-danced behind the footlights that were strung along edge of the stage. This was the first act of a minstrel show known as *The Minstrel Line*.

The second act was known as the *Olio*, which occurred after an intermission where variety acts performed in front of a painted backdrop . With and without blackface, such performers "roasted" issues and political figures of the time. This portion of the minstrel shows eventually evolved into vaudeville.

The third portion of the program was a One-Act Musical that emulated a popular novel or play and starred blackfaced characters known as *Jim Crow* and *Zip Coon*. The former, a country bumpkin that was regularly humiliated and the latter, a city slicker of sorts who usually got his confidence summarily destroyed.

Minstrel shows began in America in the early 1840s with a group known as the Tyrolese Minstrel Family who toured the country with traditional European folk songs. Dan Emmett's *Virginia Minstrels*, a blackface group, performed at the popular Bowery Amphitheater in 1843 in New York City.

This four-man group would sit in a semicircle offering songs, dances, and comedy of Negro caricatures that mark the beginning of minstrelsy. The Virginia Minstrels introduced the songs "Polly Wolly Doodle" and "Blue Tail Fly" and toured the U.S. and Europe, becoming the most popular stage productions in America. By the late 1800s there were many minstrel groups performing.

STEPHEN FOSTER'S MINSTREL SONGS:

CAMPTOWN RACES
MY OLD KENTUCKY HOME
O SUSANNA
OLD FOLKS AT HOME

JAMES BLAND'S MINSTREL SONGS

CARRY ME BACK TO OLD VIRGINNY
OH! DEM GOLDEN SLIPPERS
THE EVENING BY THE MOONLIGHT
HAND ME DOWN MY WALKING CANE

JAMES BLAND WROTE OVER 700 MINSTREL SONGS. HE WAS THE STAR PERFORMER WITH THE CALLENDER-HAVERLY MINSTRELS IN 1881 AND WAS KNOWN AS THE PRINCE OF NEGRO SONGWRITERS HE GAVE COMMAND PERFORMANCES FOR QUEEN VICTORIA AND THE PRINCE OF WALES. "CARRY ME BACK TO OLD VIRGINNY" IS NOW THAT STATE'S OFFICIAL SONG.

Gary Giddins: Though antebellum (minstrel) groups were white, the form developed the axiom that defines - and continues to define-American music as it developed over the next century-and-a-half: African-American innovations metamorphose into American popular culture when white performers learn to mimic black ones."

John Kendrick: Edwin P. Cristy's Minstrels eventually perfected the three-part-format that became the standard for all such shows, echoing into the future development of the American musical theater.

The Cohan and Harris' *Minstrels of 1909* was the last minstrel show to play Broadway, but minstrel traditions remained in use for decades.

When Jolson joined Dockstaders Minstrels as an "end man" in Plainfield, New Jersey, when he was twenty-three, he soon entered the time-honored fashion by stealing the show from the star - Dockstader himself. The spot before the end was for Dockstader, but, by the time Jolson had finished his solo, the audience belonged to him. Dockstader learned that fact quickly:

"Well, folks, I knew the kid had it, but I guess I just didn't know how much he had. Maybe he should have followed me."

Variety featured Jolson as a star in Dockstader's: "Dressing neatly in evening clothes of faultless cut and of the new color called 'taupe,' Jolson offers a quiet quarter of an hour of smooth entertainment....As it stands now, Jolson's offering is capable of holding down a place in any vaudeville show. He is now in the next-to-closing position in the olio of Dockstader's Minstrels, following Lew Dockstader and Neil O'Brien among others, and Jolson is making a good mile."

Lew Dockstader's Minstrels were among the best, professional and celebrated troupe of players in the business. With Dockstader, Jolson toured throughout the country and in Canada in a string of one-nighters for a year.

Jolson's apprenticeship in Dockstader's Minstrels paid off by familiarizing him with the art of showmanship and the rudiments of ragtime and mammy songs, the fashionable-style vaudeville music of his time, that was performed by by both black and white artists. Dockstader was his stepping stone to the big-time, working for the

Shubert Organization. He left Dockstader to join I.P. Wilkerson's Minstrels of Today, only to return to Dockstader a few months later, having to complete his contract, followed by a short period in various vaudeville shows, and then another, even shorter time with Dockstader until his manager, Arthur Klein, obtained his release from the Dockstader contract.

Jolson's days in vaudeville were numbered. During the following year he was to join with Shubert at the brand-new Winter Garden Theater in the first of many legitimate theater and musical-comedy successes. His education as a polished performer now complete, Al Jolson was ready for the big-time. He was soon to become the 20th Century's biggest name in entertainment.

Jolson in *Go Into Your Dance* Blackface Review - 1935

FINDING GERSHWIN'S SWANEE

Lyricist Irving Caesar: "One day Al Jolson hosted a midnight party after a Winter Garden performance. Buddy DeSylva invited his fellow songwriter George Gershwin. Buddy asked George to play for Jolson, and so he played the song "Swanee", among some others. Jolson adopted it at once and introduced it within three or four days, and the rest is history."

Al Jolson made "Swanee" the biggest hit that George Gershwin ever had. Jolson popularized it at the Winter Garden shows and then in a touring company of his revue "Sinbad" during 1920.

SWANEE

Irving Caesar and George Gershwin

VERSE
I've been away from you a long time
I never thought I'd miss you so
Somehow I feel
Your love was real
Near you I long to (wanna) be
The birds are singin,' it is song time
The banjo's strummin' soft and low
I know that you
Yearn for me too
Swanee! you're calling me,

CHORUS
Swanee! How I love ya
How I love ya
My dear ol' Swanee
I'd give the world to be

Among the folks in D-I-X-I-Even know
My Mammy's waiting for me
Praying for me
Down by the Swanee
The folks up north
Will see me no more
When I go to that Swanee shore.

Swanee! Swanee!
I am coming back to Swanee
Mammy, Mammy,
I love the old folks at home.

At the George Gershwin Memorial Concert at the Hollywood Bowl on September 8, 1937, Al Jolson sang "Swanee."

Jolson and Gershwin - 1919

WINTER GARDEN

SHUBERT THEATRE CORPORATION, LESSEE
Direction of LEE & J. J. SHUBERT

Winter Garden Sundays

He would call out to the theater crew, "Bring up the house lights!" then go to the edge of the stage, sit down, with his legs dangling, loosen his collar and tie, and go into his routine of songs and patter. This was considered brash, brazen, and to some, presumptuous, since theater folks were expected to keep their place behind the footlights. According to many, Jolson defied tradition and good theater manners.

Al Jolson will be fondly remembered for his Sunday-night concerts held for show people and other audiences at the Shuberts great showplace, The Winter Garden Theater, a practice he began soon after his first performance at that brand-new theater in April of 1911.

AL JOLSON:

"Many stars jump into the limelight overnight. That wasn't my experience. I had to serve my apprenticeship in small vaudeville houses, graduating later to big vaudeville circuits, and from them to the Winter Garden shows.

"Every performer has one device he thinks helps him. The surest way to kill me off would be to make the stage about ten feet wide where I would have to stand in one place.

"Many people see a Winter Garden show so often they get to know the jokes by heart. When they have them down pat, they bring their friends; and then as soon as I start a joke, they spring the finish of it. So every fortnight I have to change my jokes."

Gilbert Seldes, The Seven Lively Arts Magazine, 1912:

"This galvanic little figure, leaping on it and shouting, yet always essentially dancing and singing, was the concentration of our national health and gaiety. In 'Row, Row, Row,' he would bounce upon the runway, propel himself by imaginary oars over the heads of the audience, draw equally imaginary slivers from the seat of his trousers, and infuse into the song something wild and roaring and insanely funny."

Henry Pleasants, Musical Historian.

"He was more orator than vocalist, a characteristic demonstrated again and again in his excursions into straight declamation. It was almost as if he found the tune inhibiting."

Jolson cashed in on his fame at the Winter Garden, no doubt. He was different. He could give tremendous bounce to a song with his off-hand treatment of vowels and diphthongs. He was a very strong performer and arrested his audience from the start. And he slurred, rather than stick to the correct pitch, much like his cantor father did in Jewish ceremonial chants. This lent color and interest to his singing style once it was converted to a type of slurring, something most straight singers of his day avoided to escape criticism. He also liked to shout out to the band, saying things like "C'mon...get hot," accomplished during momentary musical rests, while he snapped his fingers and twisted his lip and shifted his hips and feet in a special dance.

Al Jolson perfected vitality and adventure in singing that would be passed on to singers that followed, like mid-career Sinatra, early Bing, Darin, Frankie Laine and all the others.

The Winter Garden was the ideal showcase, and the timing just right for Jolson to jump-start a career now that he had paid the piper during preceding years as an apprentice in vaudeville and in various associations with experienced partners, including his brother, Harry.

The Winter Garden would be synonymous with Jolson. It was his home, his turf, his mask, and his great success. First: *La Belle Paree* in 1911, *The Whirl of Society* in 1912, *Honeymoon Express* in 1913, *Dancing Around* in 1914, *Robinson Crusoe, Jr.* in 1916, *Sinbad* in 1918, a revised *Bombo* in 1923 (after a run at the Jolson's 59th St. Theater), *Big Boy* in 1925, as a guest star in *Artists and Models* in 1926, and in film, *The Singing Fool* in 1928, and in film, *Big Boy* in 1930. What a run!

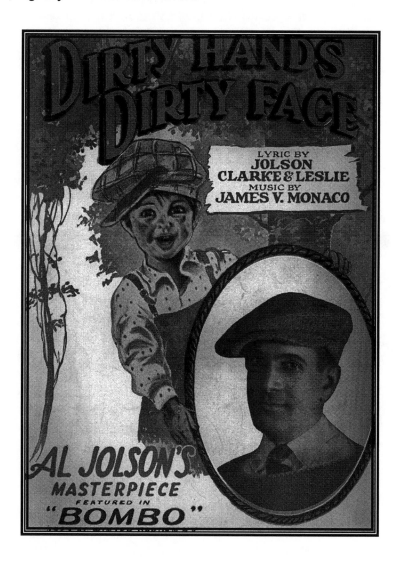

Fracturing the English Language
Linguistic Misdemeanors

AL JOLSON contrived a unique way of pronouncing and dismembering words contained in his songs and elsewhere all throughout his lifetime whether singing or just talking . Very musical,

he would whistle and bend words to fit his moment, improvising much like a jazz musician, refusing to stay on course, but always coming back. He made mincemeat of the English language and his fans loved it.

Henry Pleasants, Music Historian: "Therein lay the secret of Jolson's greatness. Therein, too, lay the root of some of his musical and linguistic misdemeanors. He loved words and his maltreatment of them was a kind of smothering with affection. He would embrace a word, squeeze it, hug it, press it to his heart, and release it reluctantly. He could milk them for more than they could yield."

John Crosby - Critic. "He has an odd style of speech wherein he managed to eliminate consonants almost entirely. In Alexander's Ragtime Band radio broadcast

he sings,'Come awn an' heah, come awn
an' heah...de bes'ban' in de lan.' and also
something about looking 'troo de deep
tangle'wil'wood.'"

Notable Examples:

Singing became "*singin'* "

You - became either *yoo, yew or yuh*: "*Yew-you're drivin' me*
crazy."

Nothing became *nuthin'* and haven't became ain't as in: "*You*
ain't heard nuthin' yet!"

Melody became mel-o-dee: "*Rockabye your baby with a*
Dixie mel-o-dee."

Yes, Sir! became "*Yessuh!*"

California became *Ca-lif-forn-yah!*: "*Ca-lif-forn-yah here I*
come.."

The became da and you became ya, and with became wid :
"*Wid all the soul dat's in ya.*"

About became 'bout and this became dis as in : "*Dis evenin',*
'bout a quarter to nine."

You became Ya and Old became ol' : "*...how I love ya. my*
dear ol' Swanee."

Virginia became Ver-gin-yah. "*...and swing it from Ver-gin-*
yah."

My translated to mah: " *Come see Erle and mah two little*
kids."

Just a Little became "*Jus' a Liddle*"

Got them became "*Gottem*"

Something became sumpin' "*Ya know sumpin!*"

Get become Gits *"After I gits back to California!"*

The becomes Da. *"Da water feels good!"*

That becomes Dat " *It's just dat most of 'em write like dat."*

Want you to becomes wantya: *"I wantya t'meet my wife."*

For becomes "f" : *"See you later, f'not gettin' up."*

PART TWO

Hard At Work

Going From Rags to Riches

Go Into Your Dance - 1935

Vaudeville

The Greatest Live Entertainment

Vaudeville - Stage entertainment offering a variety of short acts such as slapstick turns, song-and-dance routines, and juggling performances.

Vaudeville: *alteration of Old French vaudeville, occasional or topical, light popular, possibly short for chanson du Vau de Vire, song of Vau de Vire, a valley of northwest France. dialectal vauder, to go + virer, to turn.* **American Heritage Dictionary**

After the Civil War, Tony Pastor's Music Hall, situated on the Bowery, was America's leading variety theater. In 1881 it moved uptown to 14th St. Pastor's type of entertainment led to vaudeville and burlesque and eventually the Broadway revue.

Bobby Clark and "Gypsy" Rose Lee

When Uncle Miltie performed his outrageous slapstick comedy on *The Texaco Star Theater*, a one-hour, Tuesday night television show on NBC that aired in the early fifties, everyone realized it was the last showcase, the beginning of the demise of vaudeville turned from the live stage to the television screen. I was there working at NBC and recall the old-time acts of Eddie Cantor, Harry Richman, Sophie Tucker, Bert Lahr, Abbott & Costello, and other notable veterans rehearsing with "Mr. Television," as he was known. Berle would rehearse them and direct every step, every joke, and every song, a true show business dictator. Most were happy to get work, since the vaudeville stages had been closed down, so they put up with his roughhouse direction.

During the live presentation someone out of camera range backstage would shout "Makeup!!!" and Milton Berle would receive a bag full of flour in his face or over his head usually from a midget. Feigning surprise, Berle would seem disoriented and then it would happen again. Well, that was television vaudeville. So was CBS's *Ed Sullivan Show* with its endless dog acts, circus acts, oddity acts and appearances of almost every viable performer of the time that was once the staple of vaudeville shows. To many Americans watching television, variety shows were a continuation of vaudeville and burlesque shows they were once able to attend in their own home town theaters.

> *Vaudeville differs from burlesque, although one has juxtaposed the other over time. However, burlesque entertainment was more risqué and revealing, featuring extensive nudity and even x-rated acts.*

Vaudeville theaters featured performers in their own acts: jugglers, acrobats, buffoons, clowns, comedians, animal acts, singers, dancers, actors in melodramatic sketches. With the exception of burlesque houses scattered throughout mostly the larger cities, vaudeville was the standard of entertainment in America. Vaudeville catch-phrases "direct from New York" was insurance for "socko" attendance at small-town theaters.

In the period from 1900 through the 1940s the infamous Shubert Brothers would define their empire of theaters as performing "legit," meaning plays and musical attractions, as distinguished from burlesque, vaudeville, and motion pictures.

By 1911, Al Jolson was a popular vaudeville star. Before

Bing Crosby attracted attention, and radio and sound films came into their own, Al Jolson had already held the title of America's Greatest Entertainer. And it all began for him in vaudeville; and it continued on Sunday nights at the famed Winter Garden Theater in New York where he achieved extraordinary fame.

Unlike other performers of his time, Jolson was ten times larger than life. In his time he had it *all*. And I mean all! He danced, he related funny stories and jokes, he involved his audience, and sang like no one had ever done before him. He acted and dressed up in blackface , a tool he developed from his minstrel days for his characterization of "Gus," his on-stage personality.

Enter Burlesque

Burlesque owed its beginnings to the circus, minstrel shows, beer and dance halls, and honky-tonks. It's first producers came from the circus and minstrel shows, deriving its songs, gags, and choruses. Known legitimate players, along with attractive girls, performed without nudity, but only to build up the otherwise steamy productions.

In America, the earliest known burlesque shows were performed in 1868. The troupe was Imported British Blondes, who arrived in New York from England, led by Lydia Thompson and her chorus line of hefty blondes. Lydia would augment performances for the crowd with bawdy songs, and the girls wore ruffled bloomers. Noticing that men had a weakness for such glamour, true American burlesque shows began to evolve.

Producers would combine lady minstrel shows, vaudeville, and musical parody into one format they called "burlesque." The price was up to fifty cents to see one of Michael Leavitt's famous shows. The shows rotated throughout America on a circuit (wheel) system. This system reduced the chance of a burlesque troupe being left stranded in an isolated town, which often happened in regular theater tours. The shows always emphasized girls as their main ingredient, so burlesque easily flourished.

By 1906, a season consisted of 40 weeks and employed two thousand performers in thirty-three theaters. By 1912 it increased to over 100 theaters and five thousand performers. Featured were spectacular wardrobes and beautiful girls. It was estimated that burlesque consisted of 25 percent talent, 25 percent sex,

and fifty percent exploitation. Standard burlesque entertainment in some theaters consisted of cooch dancers and employed runways in all the theaters.

Although most burlesque shows received poor reviews, they continued to remain popular and profitable. The Minsky Brothers were very successful with their large choruses featuring thirty girls per show, and they, too, maintained a runway. The Minsky's, Abe, Billy, Herbert, and Morton, were very successful producing both burlesque and vaudeville productions.

Gypsy Rose Lee, the reigning queen of burlesque, eventually signed a contract with the Shubert Brothers in 1936 to appear in their Ziegfeld Follies on the legitimate stage, giving up $2000.00 a week earned in burlesque to receiving a piddling

Bits of Old-Time Burlesque Trivia

- One theory suggests that G-strings were named for the lowest string on the violin. Another name for a G-string was "Gadget."
- The stooge comic, who takes the falls, was known as the "third banana."
- The woman delivering lines in the skits was known as the "talking woman."
- Skits were called "bits."
- To expose any part of the body was called "flashing."
- To be told to do the "Boston version" meant for you to clean it up.
- To be told to do the "Sunday school show" meant that the cops or the censors were in the audience.
- The strut before the strip was called the "trailer."
- To tell a gal she had a "swell setup" meant that you thought she had a good figure.
- A house-singer or off-stage crooner singing strip numbers was called a "bust developer."
- A "cover-up" was a concealed lapse during bits for someone who may have forgotten a line.
- When a bit was unfunny, it was often said to "lay eggs."
- A provocative stripteaser was called "the snake type."
- When the comics couldn't get laughs out of an audience, the expression "the asbestos is down" would often be used.
- When a performer was involved in a show that other performers thought was no good, there were to expressions used to describe the performer with the lesser talent: "A guy's from Dixie" or "A guy's from hunger."
- The top-floor dressing room in the theaters was called the "sleeper jump."
- The owner was called "the money guy."
- And, of course, every fan of burlesque knows that when a drummer makes a rim-shot during a striptease number, that's called "catching the bumps."

$250.00 a week with the Follies. That is how important it was for established, successful burlesque performers to step-up to "legit" theatrical performing.

In 1937, due to reforms, when burlesque stripper Sally Rand performed at the New York Paramount theater, she was ordered to wear panties instead of a "G" string. Stripteasing in nightclubs, theaters, and cabarets, became limited, and burlesque diminished in New York and other states mostly due to lawsuits and complaints that prompted new laws, causing theater and liquor licenses to be revoked.

Vaudeville and burlesque provided a livelihood for thousands of performers, musicians, stagehands, ushers, producers, candy butchers, and, even censors. The golden days of this form of entertainment virtually ended with the proliferation of motion pictures, radio, and television.

Al Jolson was brought up in this world at just the right time. He rode the wave into the world of vaudeville where he established his lasting fame.

"A word about whispering and talking in theaters: When people

cough, come in late, and do the hundred and one things an audience does do, they are making it mighty difficult for a performer to do his job. They have no idea how disturbing these things are." **Al Jolson**

Ed Wynn, The Great Comedian in the Shubert *Passing Show* of 1916

The Shuberts

In 1920 there existed five basic forms of public entertainment, known as *show business* to insiders of the time. With no television, radio, or worthy motion pictures at hand, there existed endless tried-and-tested operettas imported from Europe, some which were Americanized, adapted or translated from, and a variety of legitimate staged plays and musical comedies with weak plots composed of tenors, girls, and comedians performing specially written material and hastily written songs; revues with a built-in composite of songs, skits and limited dance acts, and always scantily-clad girls, often paraded on stage or down runways with no clothes at all. Down the ladder were ubiquitous vaudeville theaters, and below that burlesque shows, and at the very bottom

J.J. Shubert and Jolson in Paris, 1921. A Reconciliation.

there existed a variety of small town circuses that roamed from city to town to village, all across America, showcasing animals, clowns, trapeze artists, and freaks of every kind.

Then came the intrepid Shuberts, Sam, Jake, and Lee,

and everything changed. The three very strange Shubert Brothers had emigrated to America from Czarist Lithuania in 1882, the same place Al Jolson was born. The family settled in Syracuse, New York. Early on the brothers became entrepreneurs working in local theaters in various positions. They were literally financed by a Syracuse, New York haberdasher who was impressed with their talents while managing their fledgling, upstate enterprises. By their late twenties the Shuberts had gained personal control of many theaters in major cities. In 1900 they invaded New York City on a shoestring. Once on firm ground, they challenged the greatest monopoly in the history of the theater who dictated terms and bookings, and totally controlled everything and just about everyone in show business, the infamous and feared syndicate of Klaw and Erlanger.

Lee Shubert

The Shubert attack was a declaration of war upon the industry. They leased numerous theaters, put on myriad cheap productions and gradually acquired a chain of theaters stretching from the Atlantic to the Pacific, and in their wake, forced producers and stars to throw in the sponge, and within 25 years had amassed a net worth of about one-half billion dollars.

The enormously successful, but strictly quirky, Shubert Brothers partnership then known as the Messrs. Shubert, (and sometimes as Lee Shubert Presents, J.J.Shubert, or Sam S. Shubert), were literally responsible for Al Jolson's and other great stars' elevation to enormous success, as they provided the theater, the financial backing, the musicians and props.

They shrewdly allowed Jolson to regularly break away from cast, story, and music of a show, encouraging and permitting him to interpolate new, fresh, but unrelated songs into a show at any time during its run, with musical material written by other than the show's original composer, performed in a long list of Shubert Productions. Jolson was the Shubert's biggest money maker for ten straight years. He made millions for them in a time when millions were millions.

Fred Astaire and sister Adele

Fred Astaire speaks:

"The Shuberts would draft all of their stars from different

productions in nearby cities as well as New York to appear at the Sunday Night Concerts at the Winter Garden. Here is a typical Sunday-night program:"

> *Al Jolson*
> *Willie & Eugene Howard, Fanny Brice*
> *Irene Franklin & Burt Green, Charlie Ruggles*
> *Frank Fay, Fred & Adele Astaire*
> *Ben Bernie & Phil Baker ,Whiting & Burt*
> *Harry Rose, Harry Carroll*
> *Hale & Patterson & Original Dixieland Jazz Band*
> *The Winter Garden Beauties*

"That's what it was like in New York. And these Al Jolson shows usually ran longer. Adele and I learned much to further our education and Broadway experience by these engagements."

Typically, however, the Shuberts tried treating Jolson just as shabbily as they did to many other noted performers, producers, actors, musicians, and composers. But, Jolson was not an easy pushover.

J.J.: (To Al Jolson after he asked J.J. Shubert for a raise.) "But that's more money than the President of the United States makes! **I won't pay it!**"

Al: "Okay! Go get the President to sing 'Mammy.'"

Besides constantly battling with the monsters Klaw and Erlanger, the Shuberts, out to make money the good old American way, regularly and outrightly tried to cheat and chisel almost everyone who worked for them or conducted business with them or through them. They regularly dishonored or ignored contracts, consistently operating their business by filing frivolous lawsuits and invoking disputes in almost every aspect of show business. In order to protect themselves against this onslaught, producers, owners, investors, lease holders, theater managers, actors, dramatists, musicians and every type of stage worker, ultimately created protective organizations in the form of unions and guilds as a defense against the Shuberts that have lasted to this day.

Willie Klein, the brother's overworked attorney, was a very busy man, simultaneously handling and negotiating dozens of omnipresent litigations that were mostly settled out of court. Throughout their entire business life, the Shubert Brothers were always suing or being sued. They even fought bitterly among themselves.

Unfortunately, twenty-nine year old Sam Shubert had perished in a train crash while on the way to Florida. The remaining two brothers, J.J. (Jake) and Lee (Levi), who almost decided to give up their ventures due to the loss of Sam, (who was the oldest brother) continued on, however, to eventually develop a vast empire of theaters phenomenal even by today's standards. In 1924, after twenty years of operating with practically none of their own capitol, they owned, leased, or controlled over 1000 theaters in the United States that were involved in legitimate theater, vaudeville, musical comedy, and later, films. They, by far, possessed or controlled the largest inventory of costumes, scenery and stage equipment for theatrical use. They sold 130,000 tickets per night in all their owned or leased theaters. That represented an amount of one million dollars a week. There were 86 first class theaters and 750 regular theaters, representing over 60% of all operating theaters in the United States. Amazing!

The brothers' works became inevitably involved with dozens of big time performers: Actors; John, Ethel, and Lionel Barrymore, George Raft, Helen Hayes, Marie Dressler, Cary Grant (nee Archie Leach), Spencer Tracy, Jeanette McDonald [mostly a singer], Sarah Bernhardt, Marilyn Miller [who also sang], Lillian Russell, Nora Bayes, vocalist Ruth Etting, all around performer, legendary Bert Williams, English writer/playwright George Bernard Shaw, the original dance team of Fred and [his sister] Adele Astaire (before Ginger Rogers), composer-conductor Sigmund Romberg, song and dance man/composer/lyricist George M. Cohan, song-belters Sophie Tucker, Georgie Price, humorists Will Rogers and Frank Fay, comedians Ed Wynn, Fannie Brice, Fred Allen, Jack Benny, Eddie Cantor, the Marx Brothers, Gallagher and Shean, Jack Pearl, Willie Howard, Bob Hope, and George Jessel, vaudeville acts Clayton, Jackson and Jimmy Durante, orchestra leader and performer Ted

Lewis, composer/lyricist Irving Berlin, Scotland's great star Harry Lauder, the one and only Mae West, and even burlesque star "Gypsy" Rose Lee herself, among endless other acts, musicians and composers, and, of course, the greatest of them all, Al Jolson.

In a nutshell, it is safe to report the Shuberts had assembled the dominant theatrical empire of the United States and the world. They produced 25% of all plays and controlled 75% of all theater tickets. Additionally, they were seated on the original corporate boards of film studios Metro-Goldwyn-Mayer and United Artists. Over the course of their career they jointly and severally produced 520 productions beginning in 1901 and winding up in January 1954 for an average of about 100 productions per year.

In 1911, the Shuberts great showcase next to the famed Hippodrome was the Winter Garden Theater, which opened for the first time featuring a young, brash, Broadway newcomer named Al Jolson starring in a show called La Belle Paree. It would become the first of Jolson's long list of big hits.

Avoiding the Rain in Shubert Alley
From *The Brothers Shubert* by Jerry Stagg

"From the elevator of the Shubert Theater, you could make your way under the marquee that projects a few feet above Shubert Alley, heading towards 45th Street. From the marquee of the Shubert, you could move under the marquee of the Plymouth Theater (Alley-side), then around in front of the Plymouth, and still be untouched by a drop of rain, then proceed to the shelter of the Booth's marquee. After watching the traffic, you may dart swiftly across the street to the Imperial, open the door of the Imperial, walk the long lobby, then through the theater to backstage, and out the stage door, and turn sharply and enter Dinty Moore's Restaurant. No one will even get damp."

To prove the existence of the Shuberts' continuing war with anyone for almost any reason, especially when money was involved, they actually tried to stop the 1947 film *The Jolson Story* from opening at the Radio City Music Hall in New York, as sort of a counterattack upon Columbia Pictures for past grievances, so they sued Columbia. They wanted $500,000.

According to Stagg:

"Their reasoning was that they had employed Jolson for many years. He had appeared in eight separate Shubert hits at the Winter Garden, not to mention the Shubert theater they had graced with his name, Jolson's Ambassador Theater in New York City.

"But it was Jake Shubert's Winter Garden Theater that was their major complaint. They humbly petitioned the court that Columbia not be permitted to show any part of the 'Winter Garden' in the film, inside or out, or to use the name 'Winter Garden,' or to mention 'Shubert' unless they received Shubert permission and were paid 'valuable consideration,' that is, one-half-million dollars."

A Young Joan Crawford in a Shubert Show

The case was eventually thrown out of court, even though the Shuberts added the startling and unexpected claim that *The Jolson Story* was originally based on a script called *The Winter Garden*, to which they owned the rights. They didn't. The author had retained the rights.

There is one more story we can't escape telling involving the Shuberts, Al Jolson, and Georgie Price. Turn the page.

The Continuing Tale of Georgie Price

    Georgie Price, who was doing well enough as a vaudeville star, was suddenly sought out by Lee Shubert to be groomed as a replacement for Al Jolson. The Shuberts felt that Jolson was becoming disgruntled, even though is was caused by selfish actions of both Jake and Lee Shubert, like charging Jolson $ 500.00 for costumes for a show when Al knew the costumes were Shubert inventory and worth no more than $ 50.00. Al was making too much money, so they needed to replace him. The fact that Al made millions for them, more than anyone else had, meant nothing to them. However, Price didn't realize what was in store for him. The Shuberts cajoled Price with dinners, acquired him an apartment across from Times Square, and acceptance as though a member of their family. They upgraded his dressing room and offered him $350.00 a week in a five-year contract. At the time George Price was one of the best-selling recording stars of "His Master's Voice" RCA Victor Records.

The offer was bumped up to $ 500.00 a week, but Georgie held fast, wondering what they were up to, not exactly trusting the Shuberts. He held tight and the offer was upped to $ 750.00, featured billing, and extra fees to be negotiated for any Sunday night special shows.

Georgie Price signed. His fate was sealed. They generously introduced him to, and married him off to, a great showgirl and even promised to take them to Europe, all expenses paid. Then, suddenly they asked him to sign a release for no pay on his contract while he was in Europe, and had him finish his contract on a foreign vaudeville stage.

When they issued him the tickets for the steamer to Europe, they asked for $ 750.00. Shubert was already reneging on his promise to take them as his guests, denying he ever made the offer. Georgie worried about paying for the expenses of the trip, but he had no choice now.

Meanwhile, Lee Shubert had carefully worked on Jolson, who wasn't easy to deal with, despite his reputation as being an easy negotiator, and sometimes an equally nasty adversary. But, he finally signed Jolson, so their crisis was over and they no longer required the services of one Georgie Price after all.

Suddenly, without notice to Price, they relegated him to star billing according to the contract, but in almost unreadable and tiny letters. He was not featured and was reduced to the inconspicuous in the show.

The Shuberts ignored his complaining phone calls. They

became unavailable. His dressing room was situated way up on the third floor. Worried, Price sought legal help. His attorney went to bat and sent a blistering letter to the Shuberts claiming breach of contract.

Price would not appear at the low-class Central Theater and was told by the Shuberts that he was in breach of his contract. Price panicked. He had little money and was worried about his hard-earned career that the Shuberts had set out to destroy. He did not understand what had happened. He did not know they settled with Jolson.

Price sued for $ 300,000.00. The Shuberts finally caved in and set Price up in a show in Boston but, again, assigned him a third floor dressing room and had him walk on three times per show, twice in blackface and once without, with no number to perform. He was told he would just stand there on stage with nothing at all to do. They wanted to humiliate him so he would quit. However, he was performing " as directed by management" and being paid $1000.00 a week, and wouldn't give it up.

For six months this continued and Price could do little about it. He could not afford to quit. What would he do?

Then they tried to kill him with reverse action by having him tour with the Shuberts' *Passing Show*. They had him appear in thirteen scenes with eleven costume changes, sing eight songs, gave him a tiny dressing room far from the stage, and had him running, running, running. The show was a series of one-night stands going from one town overnight to another. They had him reporting to the freight yards at 3:00 AM and traveling in box cars with the scenery. It became a nasty game. He had to follow their demands or lose his contract.

Price was a well-known talent and put up with this terror perpetrated by the Shuberts, who tried to break him, and his contract. But he needed to win his personal battle against the Shuberts. They used him to replace Al Jolson. Now, they didn't need or want him, so they victimized and blacklisted him. But he held on despite acquiring an ulcer and losing much weight.

"You want to quit, George? We won't mind." the Shuberts sent notice.

Price fought back, cleverly claiming illness on a Saturday night forcing the Shuberts to refund all the ticket prices. He recovered to perform the weekly shows, but suddenly became sick on sold-out Saturday nights.

Shubert called and Price nailed him to the wall with his complaints which Shubert denied knowing anything about. "You lose...I'm not quitting, " he told Lee Shubert. Shubert gave in for a moment realizing Price was determined.

Georgie Price worked out his contract of three years that almost killed him. He settled with Shubert for a future final year after performing at the famed Palace for the Keith organization as a headliner for $ 1,750.00 per week for two years, followed by myriad vaudeville appearances. He met with great success during that in-between contract year with Keith.

As promised, Price happily returned to finish out his year with his promised own show for the Shuberts. He had assembled new songs and sketches to use for this promised event. By this time Jake Shubert acquired hate for George Price and summarily relegated him once again to a minor part in a show that ran in Detroit and starred Phil Baker - not him.

After re-invoking his trick of suddenly getting sick on Saturday night with a sore throat, Jake became furious. He barred Price from all his theaters regardless of contract. Price demanded the balance of his salary to satisfy the rest of his contract. Jake Shubert was known to have said, "I will see you in Hell first."

Price, leering at Jake Shubert in his office, promised to give him trouble, which Shubert shrugged off until Price said the trouble would be from "the government."

"What kind of talk is this?" demanded Shubert, "We treated you well." Price showed him a photostat of a check he received from Shubert written on a so-called Shubert charity fund.

Shubert became nervous, called in his attorney who perused the check and agreed to a settlement with Georgie Price for $26,000.00.

Georgie Price had beaten the Shuberts and they knew it. At last, he was satisfied.

After a short, but final stint in show business, Georgie Price became a Wall Street broker. He never forgot the viciousness of Lee and Jake Shubert.

Many years later Price, his wife and three year old son, met up with Jake Shubert in Florida. He greeted Price graciously and gleefully took his son for an outing, and deluged him with gifts, causing Price to shake his head in disbelief and wonderment.

Georgie Price could never figure the Shuberts. He must have concluded that the Shuberts considered business moves more important than anything else, but their struggle with Price was not really very memorable or remorseful to them. It was simply the way the Shuberts did business. They treated everyone badly. Georgie Price and Al Jolson were no exceptions.

There are many similar stories on file relating to those two ubiquitous entrepreneurs

Willie Howard as Charlie Chaplin and Marilyn Miller as Mary Pickford in *The Passing Show* - 1915

of show business, the brothers Shubert. This was just one of them.

Fanny Brice and Bob Hope in the Ziegfeld Follies

THE BARRYMORES

JOHN
BARRYMORE

ETHEL
BARRYMORE

LIONEL
BARRYMORE

The Competition
Legitimate Theatre

During the era of Jolson's great Broadway successes, there was much competition for attendance ticket sales, much as there is today, for live theater productions in the world of musical comedy and for major dramatic shows.

Earlier, in the late 19th century, sometimes called the Gay Nineties, musical plays began with such shows as *A Trip to Chinatown*, with notable, durable songs "The Bowery," and "After the Ball," or another choice was imported Viennese operettas. The twentieth century began with Victor Herbert musicals, Franz Lehar's works, as *The Merry Widow*, and Jerome Kern and Guy Bolton earned fame at the time with the Princess Theater musicals.

George M. Cohan

Among the big names in the legitimate theater were the Barrymores; John, Lionel, and Ethel, all who went on to great success in films. In musical comedy, George M. Cohan, one fourth of the Four Cohans, wrote words and music and starred in his own productions. The Cohans were a family who performed in vaudeville. There was father and mother Cohan, Jerry and Nellie, and the kids, Josie, and George, who became an important figure on Broadway, worked together for years, becoming one of the most popular attractions in America. George produced and starred in *Yankee Doodle Dandy* and *Little*

Johnny Jones, and composed the songs "Over There," "Give My Regards to Broadway," "Forty-Five Minutes from Broadway," "Mary's a Grand Old Name," and "You're a Grand Old Flag," selling many tickets for all his shows, stiff competition during Jolson's era.

GIVE MY REGARDS TO BROADWAY
GEORGE M. COHAN

Give my regards to Broadway
Remember me to Herald Square
Tell all the gang at forty-second street
That I will soon be there
Whisper of how I'm yearning
To mingle with the old time throng
Give my regards to old Broadway
And say that I'll be there 'ere long

Jerry, Nellie, Josie and George M. Cohan

Willie Howard and Marilyn Miller were in *The Passing Show* of 1915, a Shubert Brothers' production, wherein Howard emulated Charlie Chaplin and the beautiful Miller, Mary Pickford.

Comedian Ed Wynn appeared in Rudolph Friml's *Sometime* in 1918. Mary Ellis and Dennis King were the stars of *Rose-Marie* in 1924, singing "Indian Love Call" in an enduring show that was extremely popular.

Peggy Wood, who later played the lead in *I Remember Mama* on television, was serious competition in the production *Maytime*, by Sigmund Romberg.

ROSE OF WASHINGTON SQUARE

Song

Lyric by
Ballard Macdonald

Music by
James F. Hanley

As   by

FANNY BRICE
in the new
Ziegfeld Midnight Frolic

atop the
New Amsterdam Theatre
New York.

Price 60 cents

MUSIC
PUBLISHERS

When Jolson was busy captivating audiences in the 1921 production *Bombo*, Marilyn Miller captivated her own following in *Sally*, followed by another success *Sunny*, both big box office hits for the prolific star.

Showboat was killer competition for Jolson's Broadway seats in *A Night in Spain*. Helen Morgan, Edna May Oliver, Francis X. Mahoney, and Charles Winninger as Cap'n Andy starred in this early blockbuster.

In 1933, while Jolson was idle on Broadway, Bob Hope was grabbing ticket sales away from the competition for the show *Roberta* that also starred Sidney Greenstreet and Ray Middleton.

The Barrymore family dominated in a wide variety of Broadway dramas that included Ethel in *Kingdom of God* and *Scarlett Sister Mary*, and Lionel in *The Claw*, and starred in a run of successful shows over many years.

Ethel Barrymore

Meeting
John Barrymore
By Ervin Drake

AL JOLSON, describing his acting ability in the film Mammy, when playing a drunk: "I say this openly, for publication--there isn't anyone, not even Barrymore, could have played that scene better."

An Older John Barrymore

Well, Jolson wasn't the greatest actor, that is certain. The great John Barrymore, who appeared in the first sound film *Don Juan* His siblings, Lionel and Ethel, were also great actors in Jolson's time.

Songwriter, producer, Ervin Drake recently told me of his encounter with John Barrymore:

"When I was still sixteen years of age (1935), John Barrymore was staying at the home of Elaine Barrie at 280 Riverside Drive in New York City. Coincidentally, my family resided in the same building. Miss Barrie and my older sister Beatrice were close friends. As a matter of fact, Miss Barrie's mother (Mrs. Louis Jacobs) arranged to gather up Mr. Barrymore at a hospital where he had recovered from pneumonia, and put him up at their apartment for the better part of that late Spring and early Summer. Later, when the well-convalesced Mr. Barrymore invited Elaine and her mother to be his guests on his yacht, the Infanta, my twenty- year-old sister went along with them as a kind of chaperone. When I grew up, Beatrice recounted stories of a roisterous, sometimes violent and frightening voyage.

"In 1935, I was a Townsend Harris High School undergrad and had dreams of becoming a cartoonist. Sports, comics, anything- as long as it entailed cartooning. I had yet to study figure drawing in any formal manner, but I had a small, innate talent. On lovely Spring and Summer afternoons, I would be up on the roof with a pad of paper and pencils,

Ervin Drake

sketching either things around me or things in my mind's eye. One afternoon, a long shadow fell across my drawing of the moment and a voice that I knew asked me if I would mind a critique of my work.

"Looking up, I recognized John Barrymore. I responded eagerly that I would welcome such input. He then started to show me just where and how parts of my figure sketches were "out of drawing." He spoke authoritatively and offered to make corrections. Taking my pencil, he swiftly outlined the musculature and bone structure beneath the flesh, explaining the importance of these basics to the final representation. He told me he himself had been an artist (cartoonist) on a Hearst newspaper years before. He advised me to buy at least one book on anatomy by George

Bridgman. (Over the years I have acquired several).

"We ran into each other often on that roof, but he was less inclined to give more drawing lessons and much more into revealing aspects of his life, all aspects of it, to his new sixteen year old friend. He asked earnestly whether I had ever been down to Mexico, and, if I had, had I enjoyed the charms of the local whores in those cribs.

"Feeling insufficient, I confessed that, up to that moment, the answer was no! I had never set foot across that border, nor had I yet sampled the venereal delights of those muchachas. He even confessed to me, though I had no idea then of his prior relationships, that of all his companions, and wives, the only one he ever truly loved was Dolores Costello. (I thought I had once seen this actress he adored). He mentioned an earlier marriage to the fascinating Michael Strange (an equally fascinating first name for a woman to a teenager in 1935) but I do not recall any other comments about Miss Strange.

"Barrymore never talked down to me. It was always as if he did not know, or care, that his confidant was an authentic naïf. Thinking back on it years later, I begin to understand the unfortunate stories about him in Hollywood when he was in the presence of figures of authority, including the story about him getting very drunk in the home of a studio executive and urinating on his living room drapes. Clearly, his unusual response was impossibly arrogant and insulting. But not with those he found unchallenging. Like this, then little boy. For me, he was a darling human being and I am fond of those fragmentary recollections.

"Although I was to practice cartooning at my college, CCNY, I never did choose it as my life's work, opting for the life of a songwriter instead."

Ervin Drake is the composer of "It Was A Very Good Year," "I Believe," "Al Di La," "Father of Girls," "Come to the Mardi Gras," "Perdido," and other great songs.

Making Decca Records
For Jack Kapp

Jack Kapp was president of Decca Records and a guy who loved all his performers. Kapp loved Bing Crosby and Al Jolson; Guy Lombardo, The Andrews Sisters, The Mills Brothers, and Louis Armstrong.

Jack implored Jolson to record his old-time hits for the then younger generation. Jolson hedged, that is until he began his radio shows and captured America with his filmed biography, *The Jolson Story*.

> *Jolson in 1919: " ..I don't like making phonograph records. In order to make the best possible record, you have to sing right into the mouth of the horn. That means that I have to stand quietly in one spot while I sing - which is a practical impossibility for me. In fact, the first records I made were poor because I demanded that I be allowed to run around the room(studio), snap my fingers, throw back my head and make any movement I wished to make. The studio guys tried to explain why I couldn't, but I would not listen."*

In 1934, only 12 million records were sold in America. By 1947 that figure grew to 300 million. Some recording executives swore phonograph records were going the way of player-piano rolls. At this point Jack Kapp founded Decca Records. Bing Crosby trusted him completely and he was loyal to Kapp. Kapp had Crosby record with every known artist and vocalist in the business at the time, virtually becoming responsible for Crosby's great recording career that included a mixed cornucopia of blues, cowboy, Irish, patriotic, ballads, classics, religious, Hawaiian and country material to help Crosby keep alive as a recording artist.

It was the sheer volume of recordings that helped Crosby's rising star, long after the average performer was washed up. The association was kept between them for over 20 years.

Kapp always kept his pulse on what the public wanted. Kapp decided to record the songs from *The Jolson Story.* Sound tracks of the movie's leading songs were sent to him from the studio. He prepared an album and waited. When he viewed the final version of the film at a private showing, he discovered they had left out the most beautiful and sentimental song from those sent to him: "The Anniversary Song" that Jolson sings for his parents at the end of the film.

Bing, Jack Kapp and Harold Arlen

"I am sitting there with my wife, and I am crying. The songs are a flashback for me from when I was a little boy. Then I hear this wonderful song, I jump up and I run from the projection room. I tear my hair. The song Jolson sings to his parents; I don't even know its name. They didn't think it important enough to let me hear it on the sound tracks.

"So I rush out to the coast by plane. 'What are you doing to me?' I ask the movie people. 'You've left out the biggest song in the picture, and I haven't got it in my album.'"

Jack Kapp, master recording executive and premier artist and repertoire man for Decca Records, hustled Al Jolson to a recording studio to sing the missing "Anniversary Song," and more than a million records of it were sold in a year.

> *By 1948, the year's top selling popular record albums were: #1 Stan Kenton's "A Presentation of Progressive Jazz," and # 2 "Al Jolson Volume III" and # 12 and # 13 were Decca's "Al Jolson Album" and "Al Jolson's Souvenir Album." In between were albums by Glenn Miller, Bing Crosby, Perry Como, and a Theme Song Album of the Big Bands.*

Rose of Washington Square

The Radio Shows

Al Jolson instantly thrilled some 20 million radio listeners on the opening of his Kraft Music Hall show in the fall of 1947. That set a record for a "new" radio performer. Al had been absent from his audiences for such a long time that many younger listeners thought he was a newly discovered talent performing a new style of singing. Of course, many more knew it to be a recall-to-life of the greatest Broadway star of the past, Al Jolson.

They recognized the vigorous, carefree and unabashed delivery that had made him world famous some thirty years earlier when he virtually held New York City theatergoers in the palm of his hand when performing at the famed New York showcase, the Shuberts Winter Garden Theater. After the show, old friend and rival George Jessel had this to say:

"Explaining Jolie's dynamics would be like trying to capture the power of the ocean by putting it up in bottles."

In 1947, with his hair grown thin, a few years beyond sixty, and recently married to glamorous, twenty-five year old, Erle Galbraith, Al had eternally recaptured his own youthful exuberance when he was placed in front of a live audience. As long as he was close to an adoring public, he was content.

Outfitted in a signature turtleneck sweater, there he was again, rehearsing a full orchestra and a full chorus, inexhaustible, bouncing around the studio like he, too, was only twenty-five. Funny, Al was never sure of his age. Was he then sixty-one or sixty-five?

Earlier, when he would urge his father to certify his age, his father would say: "Asa, you are forty-eight."

With Radio Announcer Ken Carpenter

"But, how do you know for sure, Papa?"

"It's very simple. Last year you were forty-seven."

Al was earning $7,500 a week from Kraft. That's how well he was respected in 1947 just before the Technicolor extravaganza *The Jolson Story* was released.

Gerald Nachman, author of Raised on Radio:

"Radio frustrated Jolson in every way;
its limited time frame cramped his style and
he couldn't take forty-five minute encores.
Inhibited though Jolson was by Radio,
his talent was so enormous that his voice
embodied the invisible Jolie and radiated

electricity. His power was reduced by half on routine variety shows, but 50 percent of Jolson was equal to 100 percent of just about anybody else. You felt his presence in every song."

Dick Haymes, Jack Kapp, Jolson and Crosby, Courtesy: Dick Haymes Society

Harry Jolson: On radio, Al found he was no longer master of his own fate. He had now come under the dictation and direction of others who compelled him to sing and speak in their own way instead of his own. Being independent financially, Al could simply quit radio in disgust and sometimes rage.

AL JOLSON: "The radio studio managers have realized they get better results out of us if we can work before people, rather than just before a mike. They have built in seats and invited audiences who bring with them that intimate thread of contact and understanding so necessary to a good performance."

Sure, the radio studio contained a live, although small audience, however the situation was clearly different. He could not push the blasted microphone aside because his voice would certainly not be heard over the air and into the living rooms of America, so he had to learn to embrace it as Bing Crosby and

Eddie Cantor, Jolson, George Burns and Gracie Allen

other radio performers had learned to before him.

In any case, he achieved tremendous ratings in the annual Hooper Radio Ratings for the 1947-48 season in the aftermath of *The Jolson Story*. He was resting comfortably in first place with a 19.0 rating. Bing Crosby followed second with 16.9. Bing didn't mind at all.

Now, in reverse order, here are the list of Jolson's radio shows:

Jolson starred on *The Kraft Music Hall* from 1947 through 1949 in seventy-one half-hour broadcasts. He usually opened each show with a short version of "April Showers." The list of guest appearances are too many to assemble here, but included just about every known singer, actor and actress

Paul Whiteman Directs Al Jolson

in the business, from Groucho Marx to Bing Crosby, and even Humphrey Bogart.

The Al Jolson Colgate Show on CBS ran a total of thirty-nine shows at 25 minutes each beginning on October 6, 1942 through June of 1943.

Shell Chateau: 1935: Jackie Hughes, Henry Fonda, Victor Young, Fanny Brice, Al Jolson and an unidentified actress. Comedy Team Al Stone and Tish Lee are in the Foreground.

The Al Jolson Lifebuoy/Rinso Show, also on CBS, ran for ninety-nine episodes beginning December 22, 1936 and ending with the March, 1939 program. All Jolson shows always had featured guests of note. This show closed at times with Al singing "April Showers." His regulars were Harry

"Parkyakarcus" Einstein and popular comedienne Martha Raye.

Al Jolson's earliest endeavor on radio began with his 1932-33 series *Presenting Al Jolson* on NBC, ending with Al singing "April Showers," followed by the first *Kraft Music Hall* shows that covered twenty-seven programs that included dramatizations of plays and movies. Paul Whiteman's Orchestra supplied the music.

Dick Haymes, Dinah Shore, Jolson and Margaret Whiting. Dick Haymes was a favorite of Al Jolson.

The Shell Chateau Radio Show of 1935 - 1936 on NBC lasted for thirty-nine weeks with Victor Young's Orchestra and the song "Golden Gate," my favorite early Jolson recording, and "Good Evening Friends" were the signature tunes performed, but sometimes it contained specially written Shell lyrics. Those were one hour shows.

All in all there were six series of broadcasts, beginning in 1922 and winding up in 1949. There were also hundreds of guest appearances on shows other than his own, notably Bing Crosby's and many other benefit shows, the famous Barry Gray Show in 1946, and *Hi Jinx*, a daily talk show with my old NBC friends Jinx Falkenburg and her husband Tex McCrary.

NBC Radio Star

Reader's Digest 1949:

"Whether he's on or off the stage, Jolson is always puttin on a Jolson production. He has the best-developed megalomania on Broadway or in Hollywood. He often talks about himself in the third person as if he were a noted historical figure like George Washington." - Maurice Zolotow

For a guy who resisted appearing in front of a mike, Al Jolson sure had a long run on the radio.

Jolson: "One reason I have kept up with radio performances without forgetting lyrics when I am on the air live is that I take no chances. Sure, I have sung 'I'm Sitting On Top of the World" a million times, but you can be certain I never go on the air without written lyrics in front of me. I have had special copy that's easy to read of the songs I perform."

Jolson with Peggy Lee

Once, news spread throughout radioland that Al Jolson had quit cold on a lucrative radio contract. Was it money? Was it illness? Was it that he ran out of steam? Did he simply walk out on his contract?

No, it was none of those reasons. It was sponsor interference in continuity: and "I couldn't stand it." said Jolson. " They wouldn't let me alone. I will never come back to radio unless I have a contract which absolutely forbids interference by sponsors." What was this really all about?

"Well, I wanted to dramatize *The Jazz Singer*," he said, "There's nothing more beautiful that that. But they just wanted me to sing songs. I wanted to dramatize incidents in my life...my courtships and other things. It would make grand radio material. But they wouldn't let me. I offered them jokes. They edited them and said they weren't funny. I'm only a human being. What more could I do?"

It seems that the powers to be wanted Jolson and nothing

else. Jolson was in love with his wife, Ruby. He had more money than he could ever spend. He needed to get back to California and spend time with his wife. Until Al married Ruby, he never had a home. He was now homesick.

It was now fifteen weeks since he'd been home, the first he had ever known. Now, when amateur, meddling sponsors thought they could tell him what to do, he decided to throw the show like a fighter giving up a fight. He stepped out of the ring, went back to his dressing room and headed for the railroad station.

But, he'll be back. That's for certain. "You ain't heard nothin' yet!"

As Jerry Wald once observed: "People might be swell manufacturers, but that didn't mean they could write gags or pick songs for Al Jolson no matter how much they paid him.

Richard Grudens with William B. Williams

"Al Jolson will be back on radio to reward all those people who made him famous." Says Jolson: "I always pay my debts."

Speaking of radio, William B. Williams of New York's WNEW show Make Believe Ballroom, once told me he ran a no-prize contest on his show pitting the Mammy Singer, The Voice (Sinatra), and Der Bingle (Crosby) in a fifteen minute segment. Close to 2000 letters and cards were received from nine states. The final count: Jolson came in first, Sinatra second, and Bing in third place. That was in the late forties when The Jolson Story was showing.

The Barry Gray Show
Al Jolson's
Best Radio Show?

"The greatest entertainer who ever lived was singing my favorite Jolson song to me. I was beside myself. It was unbelievable."

Barry Gray

Left to Right With Barry Gray: Henny Youngman and Leo Lindy

One late night in 1946, renowned and opinionated radio personality, Barry Gray, inadvertently invited his hero, Al Jolson, to an interview on his WOR, New York radio show.

It was 3:45 in the morning, and Al had spent the evening at Leo Lindy's famous restaurant on Broadway. Leo had brought Jolson to visit the studio. When Al Jolson entered the studio, Barry described the unusual situation for his 850,000 dedicated listeners, and within minutes had Al Jolson singing his favorite song, "Rosie, You Are My Posie." From then on the show became a Jolson mini-concert.

After singing "Rosie" Gray said, "You can shoot me now," on-the-air, "Now, while I'm happy."

"Eight hundred and fifty thousand listeners at four o'clock in the morning?" Jolson raised his eyebrows, "When I was on the radio in the daytime, I never had that many listeners."

"Yes, you did!" said Gray.

For weeks before, Barry had been talking up *The Jolson Story* movie that was being featured at Radio City Music Hall in New York. Jolson had learned about it and stopped up to thank Barry. When Jolson unexpectedly appeared in the WOR studio, Barry was flabbergasted, but hastily decided to move down the hall to a larger studio to accommodate Jolson and piano-player, Harry Akst, so Jolson could sing out.

"Here I am, sitting across the table from my favorite performer, Al Jolson," Barry began describing the scene where show business people began to congregate.

Here was a completely unplanned and unrehearsed show, and for almost two hours Barry Gray had Al Jolson singing his best songs to just a piano, and sounding like he was singing at the Winter Garden, robust and joyful. He sang "April Showers," "California, Here I Come," "Swanee," "Mammy," and even "Sonny Boy" all in a full, rich voice.

Barry was just twenty-nine then and had been running his late night show for over a year. Looking back, his show is now considered the forerunner of today's talk radio.

During the broadcast, Al Jolson sang beautifully and emotionally, thrilling a small, growing live audience that included station personnel, comedians Joey Adams and Henny Youngman, restauranteur Leo Lindy, among others. Jolson recounted interesting anecdotes of his career, including the time he entered a contest of Jolson impersonators and was booed off the stage. He also recounted details of the making of The Jolson Story that included interesting anecdotes about Larry Parks and his role in the film.

Jolson also talked about how he first became interested in the idea of a runway, built through the center of the theater, when he was in Germany and saw it being used in a Max Reinhardt produced show where an apron was built out beyond the footlights over several rows of seats accommodating 80 show girls; and how it was he who performed the unique Jolson dance step on the runway scene in The Jolson Story, because, either Larry Parks could not dance

A Mature Barry Gray

well enough, or simply that Jolson wanted a live spot of his own in the film; and his certifying the debt he owed to the Sunday night performances at the Winter Garden.

"Anyway, it was a long shot and the camera was two hundred miles away," Jolson said.

There are CDs available of this two hour show, thanks to the quick thinking of a WOR engineer who was home listening to the show and taped it on acetate with his home tape recorder, or it would have been lost forever.

"Every joke I tell has to be simple and short. People sort of cock their ears to catch every word. That is a strain. So the shorter the jokes are the better." - Al Jolson

Singing For Soldiers

Walter Winchell: "He was in debt to America and never ceased paying."

Al Jolson, 1914: "I am the jest and the jingle and the song and the chuckling banter and the bright lights and the effervescent good nature of blessed Old Broadway. I am the spirit of after-eight above Forty-second, when a million mazdas fire Manhattan's lane of light and the hum of the restless taxicab is in the air."

As early as 1898, Al Jolson and his older brother Harry, as little urchins, performed for soldiers during the Spanish-American War at Fort Myer.

After the 1930s, Jolson's time had been eclipsed by those who followed him. Sound films proliferated. In music it was affable crooner Bing Crosby who became the new singing attraction. Jolson was not a great actor by any means. He was, however, a one-of-a-kind entertainer, never equaled, and he was the catalyst for every entertainer, actor, singer and comedian since his day.

He never caught up with effectively adopting microphone techniques. He

General Martin Greets Al In Panama in 1942

preferred belting out his music to a live audience as he had done on the stage of New York's Winter Garden Theater. Film and radio, as well as television, never really satisfied him. Singing for large audiences is what was needed, and he found it singing for America's fighting men and women all over the globe during two World War's and beyond. Al Jolson was the first entertainer to volunteer to entertain the troops during World War II, even before the USO sponsored other big entertainment names like Bob Hope and Bing Crosby.

Al Jolson needed those vast and appreciative audiences. Therein lay the secret of his greatness, built and cultivated many years before. He missed his long-ago performances at the Winter Garden, when he was the undisputed King.

On January 21, 1942, a little more than a month after Pearl Harbor, Jolson began his World War II tours entertaining servicemen beginning at the Jacksonville, Florida, Naval Air Station, which would be the first round of appearances that would soon take him overseas to England, North Africa and Italy.

Harry Jolson:
"Al had not waited for the USO. He had been sending telegrams and making calls to the big Army and Navy brass. He not only volunteered his services, but he demanded the right as an American citizen to go anywhere in the world where American servicemen would listen to his songs. "

Jolson was able

Al and Ben Bernie

to present his entire repertoire to the thousands of servicemen throughout the war. He sang all those great songs beginning with "Swanee," and a dozen other Jolson evergreens. He was back in top form and for a few more years he was able to be the King once again. Jolson would not accept remuneration in any form from the USO and would even pay for his own travel.

He would regularly perform more than one show when he was informed that some servicemen could not attend because the theater had limited seating.

Service personnel loved him and rewarded him with applause and standing ovations. He had entertained over 50,000 servicemen in less than two weeks. Deep in his element, for sure, he recalled old jokes and patter and they loved that, too! So, he continued performing in places like Fairbanks, Alaska; San Francisco, California; and Everett, Washington.

"In Anchorage, they told me to observe blackout regulations and put lights out. I had to laugh, for in this part of Alaska, at midnight, it is so light that you can thread a needle on Main Street." Jolson said.

They gave two performances in Anchorage, each for 1,500 servicemen. "The show lasted an hour and I almost wore the knees out of my pants singing 'Mammy.'"

When Jolson got back to New York after these stateside tours, he would call relatives of the servicemen who had given their girlfriends or parents number to him. He kept his promises and called each one, introduced himself to them, and let them know their son, husband, friend, nephew, or loved one was O.K. and lonesome for them.

> Al Jolson: "What a hole is Dakar. We had dinner of Spam, then raced by Jeep over dusty, rocky roads for 20 miles to a GI camp. Would you believe it, it started to rain just as I sang 'April Showers.'"

On a trip to islands around the Caribbean and Central &

South America, he sang for small groups from 50 to 150 and for large contingents of as many as 3,000 as well. Al Jolson became the most important moral lifter of the U.S. Army, Navy and Air force.

A Letter to the President of the United States:

Mr. President
The White House
Washington, D.C.

My Dear Mr. President,

Having been the first american performer to entertain our boys overseas in world war II, I would be most proud if you would allow me to entertain our lonely sick and wounded who are in Japan and Korea.

Jolson took his trips singing for soldiers very seriously and gave his all in every performance. His shows were held for a few in a fox hole, or for thousands in an amphitheater, or performed as a special, extra show in out-of-the-way places where the men gathered in war situations, something Jolson thoroughly enjoyed. He proved, beyond a doubt, that he was indeed, the World's Greatest Entertainer.

A few years later, it was Al Jolson who was the first to volunteer to entertain servicemen during the Korean War. Although his health was compromised during such stressful times, he nevertheless traveled to Japan and Korea to perform shows for servicemen and women.

Jolson went directly to the Korean war zones with his equally dedicated pianist Harry Akst. Now, Al Jolson was sixty-two, and he preferred singing the old songs that made him famous, favorites that he felt they too would enjoy the most.

He began the tour in Japan at a Tokyo hospital auditorium, then on to another hospital for 800 personnel. He performed special shows for bedridden soldiers. In Yokohama, he sang for almost 2,000 soldiers. The following day he was singing at several Air Force installations in airplane hangers for as many as 2,000 per show.

Harry Akst and Jolson Arrive in Tokyo Sept. 1950

Piano accompanist Harry Akst: "We did 43 shows in Korea. After each show Al would rush to the nearest Red Cross tent for oxygen to keep his strength up."

In Pusan, Korea, he sang for 1,000 men at an Evacuation Hospital mess hall. One afternoon, an outdoor show was held on a platform built in a vast swimming pool with over 4,000 personnel attending and then cheering him on.

Praising the fighting men, Jolson said: "When I talked with the men, they wanted to push beyond the 38th parallel. They were green at the beginning, that's all. Some of them went out to fight without guns. They're just babies. I saw a lot of 'em under eighteen."

The shows went on and on as they flew from base to base eventually performing for over 25,000 servicemen in 23 shows in all of sixteen days. Amazing by any standard.

During this period, exhausted by the rigor of endless

Jolson in Korea (Jim Downs on the Right With Hand Clasped Over Forearm)

performances, Al's health became a problem, but, nevertheless, while waiting for the trip back to Los Angeles, he and Harry performed a final show, Al's very last show, as it turned out, at a military hospital in Hawaii.

Jolson: "I'd hop from place to place in a helicopter. I slept and ate with the boys...any place I could find, in tents, huts. The food was very bad. Beans, chopped beets, and lots of spam. The kids were begging for entertainment. They want anybody, any name they know."

Al Jolson considered the trips singing for servicemen and women an important highlight of his life, and always declared he enjoyed the experience.

"We knew Jolson was in Korea entertaining because we read it in the *Stars and Stripes* army news. We were hoping he would come our way. We had just finished pushing the North Koreans back up the peninsula, and all of us needed a boost."

JIM DOWNS remembers Jolson in Korea.

Jim Downs lives in Ogdensburg, New York, and tells about his encounter with Al Jolson in 1950, while serving with the 74th Engineer Heavy Equipment Company where they built roads, bridges and air fields near Khesong, Korea.

Jim's folks had seen Jolson in the original film of the *Jazz Singer* when they were married in Buffalo, New York, in 1927. He grew up listening to Jolson, his parents always praising Jolson as a great entertainer.

"The day he arrived to entertain us it was a sky-blue day. I was lucky and got a seat in the front row. I watched as Al and Harry Akst and others set up the stage. Then the show began as one of the officers addressed us.

'I am pleased to introduce you to the greatest entertainer in the world, Al Jolson'" Jolson opened with a rousing "Rock-a-Bye Your Baby," "Toot, Toot, Tootsie" and "When the Red, Red, Robin

Comes Bob, Bob, Bobbin' Along," each followed by enthusiastic applause."

Jolson asked the men for song requests:

"I was sitting just behind him on the floor and shouted out "Sonny Boy," and he replied, 'You Got it, kid.' I think everybody had a lump in their throat and a tear in their eye because Al sang it with so much feeling."

The men continued cheering loudly, much to Jolson's satisfaction. Al told little stories about his friends, entertainers Bing Crosby, Bob Hope, Eddie Cantor, and songwriter Irving Berlin. Jolson sang almost every song in his repertoire for the jubilant servicemen, including the haunting "Sonny Boy."

"'Even the South Koreans knew this man was someone special singing and making people feel good. Although they didn't understand the words, they applauded as long and as loud as we did."

Jolson entertained that day for over two hours there on the front lines. "You could see the sincerity in his eyes, hear it in his voice, and feel it in your own heart. Harry Akst, his piano player, was praised by Al Jolson. They sure made a great team. Al mentioned that he could always rely on Akst as a piano player and a friend." Jolson's last song that day was "California, Here I Come," saying afterwards, "I hope and pray it won't be too long until you men get back to California."

"We applauded for a long time, it seemed. We all wanted Al Jolson to know we appreciated the show. He was in his sixties, but he was young at heart, especially when he was singing, making all of us very happy,"

Jim Downs met Al Jolson after the show. " I thanked him very much and introduced myself, telling him my parents were big fans. He said, 'Jim, thank you and your buddies for what you are doing for all of us over here.' And, 'Tell your Mom and Dad that I said hello and thanks for all their kind words.'

For Jim Downs it was certainly a special day, attending that show performed by Al Jolson in Korea over fifty-five years ago. Jim was just 21 days beyond eighteen. When Jim learned of the passing of Jolson, just thirty days or so after his performance, he said: "Our company was involved in building a bridge, so they named it *The Al Jolson Bridge*, as a tribute.

"Al Jolson will never die in my mind, because to those of us who saw and heard him entertain that day, we need only to reach back into our memory bank and he'll be there singing "Swanee" or "My Blushing Rosie" or any of his great songs. Al Jolson's greatness will never be forgotten."

Walter Winchell

Walter Winchell: "He was as much a battle casualty as any American soldier who has fallen on the rocky slopes of Korea."

An Appearance In England?

Who never performed on the commercial stage in the U.K.? Who remains popular today in England 55 years after his passing? Who toured extensively in England during World War II entertaining the troops?

Who is the most imitated entertainment personality in England today?

Who has had three books written about him by English authors?

It's not the Beatles and it's not the Rolling Stones. It's the World's Greatest Entertainer - *Al Jolson.*

Despite endless invitations during his prime, Jolson would never accept a contract to perform in the British Isles. Why? Some say it was Jolson's fear of not being accepted by British audiences. He was secure and satisfied with his following in America and was perhaps too insecure to risk performances or criticism there. This negative decision on his part went on for fifteen years.

However, traveling in Jeeps during World War II, Jolson took in Dublin, Belfast, Limerick and Glasgow, covering forty outposts and entertaining in each one. In London, on the first stop of a four week tour, they hit as many camps as possible.

"We don't care where we work, in trucks, halls, mess halls, theaters, anywhere...and that includes matinees!" Said Jolson. Although his radio shows were never commercially aired in England, Jolson could be heard over the American Forces Network when his shows were rebroadcast for American GIs stationed in Europe, especially his radio show *The Kraft Music Hall*. It was England's only access to Jolson's voice. Looking back, it was a certainty that

England would have welcomed him with their arms wide open.
It remains that England still loves Al Jolson.

Jolson Sings

FRIARS, FRIARS, FRIARS

HOW MANY CAN YOU FIND? Buddy Hackett+Eddie Cantor+Jerry Lewis+Milton Berle+Al Jolson+Dean Martin+Johnny Carson+Ed Sullivan+George Burns+Sammy Davis, Jr.+Bob Hope+Red Buttons+Walter Mathau+Cary Grant+Frank Sinatra+Arthur Godfrey+Irving Berlin+Henny Youngman+Phil Silvers+Robert Merrill+Jack Benny+Walter Winchell+Mike Todd+Sam Levinson+Don Rickles+Jimmy Durante+William B. Williams+Joe E. Lewis+Joey Adams+Cab Calloway+Howard Cosell+Jacob Javits+Art Linkletter.

The Friars Club

The Friars Club is a living, historic association of show business people.

In 1912, song and dance man George M. Cohan, who wrote "Yankee Doodle Dandy," "Give My Regards to Broadway" and "Over There" was the Abbot of the Friars:

> "The idea of the Friars Club is to boost and not to knock. I do not claim that Friars are ideal characters. If they were, they wouldn't be human. The main thing about a Friar is that he tries to do the right thing by his brother. The most we can accomplish in this world is to do the best we can for our fellowmen and this is the great big, live thing at the Friars Club - we are boosters, not knockers."

The Friars first met at a building on W. 56th Street in New York City, later at 123 West 56th Street and today at 57 East 55th Street. The Friars named their building The Monastery, because inside it resembled an old church.

Originally, the club was known as the Press Agents Association until it became The Friars Club. The first known meeting was held at Browne's Chop House in 1904. According to Friar Joey Adams, the renowned comedian who wrote the book on the Friars Club:

"A press agent makes you well-known to a lot of people who don't particularly want to know you. The difference between an actor and a civilian: when a civilian's house burns down he calls his insurance agent; when an actor's house burns down he calls his press agent."

Some names of early members and guests of honor were Broadway star and patriotic composer George M. Cohan, Italian

Laughing at the Friars - Seated: Ida and Eddie Cantor, Gracie Allen and Al Jolson: Standing: Blossom Seeley, Songwriter Harry Ruby, George Burns, Gracie Fields and Jesse Block

A Friar's Roast

L-R: George Jessel, Jack Benny, Eddie Cantor, Bob Hope, George Burns, Al Jolson and Bandleader Kay Kyser

troubadour Enrico Caruso, composer Victor Herbert, humorist Will Rogers, and Mayor Jimmy Walker.

Joey: "In June of 1907, a constitution was adopted and the fraternal order of the brotherhood of drum beaters banded together under the name of the Friars."

Some say the name Friars came from early meetings which were held in restaurants where meals consisted of fish fries, clam fries, and other fried foods, usually seasoned with Worcestershire. From this sauce the name "fryers" was hung on them and later the spelling evolved into Friars. Who really remembers? Some say they wore Friar's robes from the abandoned costume closets of a failed Broadway show. Who knows?

Joey: "A Friar is a press agent, an actor, a producer, a hoofer, a vaudevillian, a picture star, a songwriter, a promoter, a nightclub owner, a newspaperman, or he's a doctor, lawyer, Indian chief, or businessman who loves show business and show people." Al Jolson was a Friar. So was Bing Crosby, Frank Sinatra, Paul Whiteman, Irving Berlin, George Burns, Jack Benny, George Gershwin, George Jessel, Maurice Chevalier, John Barrymore, and Bob Hope.

In 1932, the Friars were flat out of business. They couldn't pay the rent. Members could not pay their dues. The Depression took over. George M. Cohan was still the Abbot.

Despite a great array of members from high up in show business, they couldn't make it. Producers Sam Harris and Max Gordon put on an emergency show with many popular stars and still they couldn't make the rent. A handful of the faithful stayed with it and moved to a loft over Lindy's Restaurant and got together in a donated suite at the Edison Hotel which was nothing more than a card room.

For a while, some meetings were held at bandleader Ted

Lewis' apartment on Central Park West with its vaulted ceilings and classy parquet floors and plenty of food. "Is Everybody happy?" Ted would cry. And they were.

In Ted's elaborate home in Elberon, New Jersey, the "boys" perhaps Jack Benny, author Damon Runyon, producer Mike Todd, and Eddie Cantor would play cards along with fifty-odd members that would wrap-up sometimes at ten the next morning, attended graciously by Lewis' butlers, waiters and bartenders.

The Friars made a comeback in 1950 when Milton Berle was television's biggest star performing as Uncle Miltie on his famed *Texaco Star Theater* originating from studio 6B at NBC's New York studios. The show was a combination of vaudeville, burlesque, and Broadway featured live on a little screen that took over the world of show business for the moment.

As an NBC page on the show and later as Ticket Division Manager issuing tickets to clients, show business people, and the general public, I frequently issued special passes for Uncle Miltie's last-minute guests, like the wives of Look Magazine's All American Football Team. In those days Berle was the indisputable King of Television and the infamous Abbot of the Friars. He was a hard-driving former vaudevillian who directed his shows single-handed while smoking giant-sized (before Castro) Havana cigars. He managed every aspect of rehearsal and literally directed the entire show on which many of his fellow Friars and vaudeville counterparts appeared as guests.

Once during a pre-show rehearsal I walked nonchalantly into the studio to rope-off seats for visiting Texaco clients when Milton summarily ordered me out of the studio, telling me to use the seventh floor access. I left fast while he was still swearing at me for interrupting his rehearsal. He was tough and mean. I remember one day during rehearsal, Eddie Cantor berated Berle for pushing around an aging Harry Richman, the great vaudeville star who was appearing on the show.

The infamous Friars Roasts have become the absolute trademark of the club. It began with the roast of comedian Jack

Benny by his famous rival, Fred Allen, followed by roasts of Bob Hope and George Jessel, who was the quintessential Friar. That's when the Friars moved into the Friary at 57 East 55th Street in New York.

Joey Adams

Joey Adams: "The Friars Club served an actor's need and pandered to his pleasure. It was his candy store, the corner pub, the factory lunchroom, the church social hall, a place to go when there was no place to go. In the old days, in-between bookings, when the actor had no place to go, he sought the haven of the Friars Club."

Then it all changed. Big show-business names moved to the West Coast along with their shows. Live network television shows and radio programs came practically to a halt in New York. The Ed Sullivan Show took a final bow, the Paramount, Strand, Roxy and Loew's State theaters went dark. The Copa closed, the Latin Quarter was gone. Big name performers Jerry Vale, Pat Cooper, Harry James, Martin & Lewis, Phil Silvers, and Sergio Franchi hitailed to Vegas. Almost everyone in show business fled to Vegas to earn their keep. It was where the action was. The small rooms, the lounges, Sinatra, and the Rat Pack with Dean, Sammy and Joey proliferated and, of course, all the girls of show business that were not performing on Broadway joined the migration.

And they moved their homes there too.

Many tired, retired guys and gals moved to Florida to vegetate and sometimes perform on the Florida circuit. Los Angeles formed their own Friars Club. Now there were two. One East and one West.

I once attended a New York Friars lunch as the guest of Jerry and Rita Vale when the Friars introduced and toasted our new book, *Jerry Vale-A Singer's Life*, which Jerry and I put together in 2001.

If you ever get the opportunity to visit the Friars in New York you will notice the chairs with the names of former Friars who now perform for St. Peter. Ben Bernie, Eddie Cantor, John Philip Sousa, W.C. Fields, Fred Allen, and our own Al Jolson.

Some Roast and other Friar's jokes:

Milton Berle

Comedian Jack E. Leonard to soft actor Hugh Herbert who was smoking a cigar: "Don't you ever inhale? Herbert zinged back: "Not with you in the room."

Milton Berle at the roast of Frank Sinatra: "We are here for one reason and one reason only. You can sum it up in one word: Fear!"

Bob Hope on George Jessel: "Georgie used to work as a producer for Darryl Zanuck at Twentieth Century. He was really the key man out there. Every time Zanuck went to the men's room Jessel handed him the key."

George Burns re George Jessel's performance with respect to the stage production of *The Jazz Singer*: " It took me apart, I cried like a baby. When he finished 'Kol Nidre' I ran backstage with tears streaking down my face to congratulate him, but his manager wouldn't let me in the dressing room saying that Jessel had all his clothes off. 'What's that got to do with it?' I complained,' Don't you know that this is not the first time I've seen a naked Jew.' "

Comedian Joe Frisco to Enrico Caruso: Addressing the great man himself before a performance: "Hey, C-C-Caruso," he nudged, "d-d-don't do 'D-D-Darktown Strutters Ball' - that's my number and I follow you.' "

Milton Berle about Sports Announcer Howard Cosell: "I'd like to say, Mr. Cosell, when the truly great names of the sports announcers are read - you'll be sitting there just listening."

Johnny Carson about comedian Alan King: "Alan has a lovely family-he's got success-he's got a lovely home-he's got his own show-and he'd give it all up in a minute for one thing - talent!"

Comedian Jack Carter about Jerry Lewis: "Jerry is a unique individual - he's the only man in the world belted in the mouth by Mahatma Gandhi"

Well, you get it, don't you? Love the Friars club?

FRIARS MEMORIES

BY SAM M. LEWIS

(Author of Jolson song "Rockabye Your Baby")

Listen my children and you shall hear
The tales of the Friars of Yesteryear
Their home was built with laughter and song
Where squabbles and hatred did not belong
The walls seem'd to echo with good cheer
Whenever an actor would appear

Breaking a jump-from God knows where
A Sunday open-an extra fare
But a trouper couldn't resist the "Bang"
To say hello-to his old gang

And here are the names you'd meet each day
One block east from old Broadway
Will Rogers-Hitchcock and Georgie Cohan
Sam Bernard and Louis Mann

Al Jolson-Dockstader-Montgomery and Stone
Victor Herbert-Gershwin and Baldy Sloan
the Mortons-James Norton and Eddie
And Willie Collier, the laughing boy
(four other verses omitted)
Sing-Here's to the Friars-here in the hall
And to those that have answered the last curtain call
To them we are thankful for many things
But mostly for "prompting us" from the wings.

Sports Fan Jolson

Al Jolson was an incurable sports fan. He couldn't be pried away from a racetrack. At professional fights he liked to sit in the press seats-close to ringside. He never missed attending a heavyweight championship and he would attend fights in honky-tonk clubs or at New York's great venue, located then at Madison Square Garden on 8th Avenue, whenever and wherever events of his interests were featured.

At Santa Anita with Ruby and Sybil Jason

When the *Los Angeles Dons* launched pro football in Los Angeles, he purchased an interest in the club and even sponsored the "Al Jolson Sonny Boys," the kid team that played during half-time.

When Joe Louis knocked out Billy Conn for the second time in New York, Jolson stayed up the night before to get his work out of the way so he could fly to the fights just to be there for the great sports event.

Jolson would root for his pick in a horse race with that booming voice that only the horse could hear despite the screaming of 70,000 fans doing the same thing.

Erle Jolson, like Ruby Keeler before her, would accompany Jolson to the California race tracks at Santa Anita and Del Mar Turf Club in Del Mar, the latter originally owned in part by Bing Crosby and actor Pat O'Brien in the days when Crosby owned and ran horses. Ruby and Al would regularly attend prize fights at the famed 2000 seat Olympic Auditorium on Grand Avenue in nearby Los Angeles, not far from their home in Encino.

Jolson and Erle at Del Mar

Al Jolson was also known to invest in the career of prize fighters. Jolson was the money behind promoter Eddie Mead's purchase of Henry Armstrong's contract in 1936.

Al Jolson was not a sports participant, but he was certainly a fan of all sports, although he was a pretty good golfer.

Al Jolson, Eddie Mead and Henry Armstrong

Poolside In Encino With Ruby

With Ruby in "Go Into Your Dance"

With Erle At Santa Anita

With Erle at the Theater

PART THREE

Wives Tales

Al Jolson and Ruby Keeler

AL JOLSON MARRIED FOUR TIMES:

Henrietta Keller	Married: 9/20/07	Divorced: 7/8/20
Ethel Delmar (Ethel's real name was Alma Osborne)	Married: 7/22/22	Divorced: 3/20/26
Ruby Keeler	Married: 9/21/28	Divorced: 2/27/40
Erle Galbraith	Married:1/16/45	Never divorced

Al Jolson first married on September 20, 1907 to Henrietta Keller whom he met in California. Almost immediately the marriage suffered from Jolson's forced wandering throughout a show business life, leaving her constantly alone, preventing the existence of an otherwise normal life due to the many highs and lows of his career. Henrietta eventually tired of Jolson's need to perform, compounded by

Henrietta Keller

his obvious disinterest in keeping a home, and divorced him in July of 1920.

Al Jolson married vaudeville performer Alma Osborne, aka Ethel Delmar, on July 22, 1922. This marriage was consummated in Maine at a vacation resort and would only last four years and one month. Again, constantly a wife left alone while her career-building husband toured and traveled, perhaps forgetting he had a wife at home, Ethel Delmar divorced him, although it was not his wish, but

Ruby

and
AL

In
California

circumstances became intolerant to his career, despite his attempts to reconcile with her.

RUBY:

Al Jolson married winsome, sweet-faced dancer Ruby Keeler on September 21, 1928 in Westchester County, New York.

Ruby Keeler: "We didn't have a big wedding. I was lucky because I'm a Catholic girl and marrying a Jewish man we were not married in the church; We were married by a Justice of the Peace. It was not a blessed marriage, just one in the eyes of the law. In the eyes of my church I wasn't married because we did not have minister of God, or a rabbi, or priest, just a Justice of the Peace." After living a hectic life in New York City, Jolson enjoyed spending time with Ruby at their ranch home in California's more sedate San Fernando Valley. They enjoyed many afternoon sessions in their swimming pool.

"...our marriage comes first--with both of us. When Ruby was making 42nd Street, I got home for dinner one night and she wasn't there. I felt like a lost pup. I was hungry all right, but I couldn't sit down alone at that empty table. When I told her how I felt, she said she'd never let it happen again. And she never did. She'd start work at seven in the morning sometimes, so as not to hold up the schedule, but she was always home to have dinner with me at six." At their Encino, California home, pianist Harry Akst would come over to rehearse with Jolson, otherwise, according to Ruby, they had little company, except for Al's brother, Harry and his wife, and once, Al's father, who came to dinner. Ruby and Al adopted one child.

Jolson enjoyed his life more with Ruby Keeler than his previous alliances. They spent a lot of time together and traveled extensively, including to Europe. In 1929, when Ruby opened on Broadway in Florenz Ziegfeld's *Show Girl* in New York, Al Jolson stood up in the audience and sang the Gershwin song "Liza" as his wife danced on stage, much to everyone's surprise:

Ruby Keeler: *"Al had heard the song a lot during*

rehearsal, a song he felt was perfect for him, so he just got up and sang it, but he did that only once."

Harry Jolson: *"Suddenly Al sprang to his feet and began singing the chorus of 'Liza' with Ruby. It was an unpremeditated, unrehearsed act and Ruby was probably the most astonished of all.*

When the song ended the audience nearly tore the roof from the building with applause and Ruby actually shed tears on the stage."

The couple performed together in the 1935 film *Go Into Your Dance* and had high expectations to perform together again. In 1937, they were featured as themselves along with Sybil Jason in Warner's *A Day at Santa Anita*, a racetrack

Ruby with Clayton, Jackson and (Jimmy) Durante in Showgirl

where they were regulars. In June of 1940, they appeared together in the stage show *Hold On to Your Hats*. While touring, competing rifts between them caused a separation which led to their divorce six months later. Ruby Keeler worked Warner Brothers' musicals in the 1930s, including her debut in *42nd Street* in 1933, in which she played a chorus girl, then went on to star in another eight musical productions. In 1971, she made a comeback on Broadway, tap dancing in *No, No, Nanette*. Some of her other films were: *Golddiggers of 1933*, *Footlight Parade*, *Shipmates Forever*, and *Ready, Willing and Able*.

"I had a little talent, but never wanted to be a star. To me, fame, success - well, it's so fleeting." Ruby always protected the name of Al Jolson to detractors whom she felt exaggerated his faults.

Born in Halifax, Canada, Ruby later married John Lowe, a developer, in 1941. They had four children. She suffered a debilitating stroke in 1974 and passed away in February, 1993, at the age of eighty-three. She will be remembered as a reminder of the great days of Hollywood musicals that spawned works by the great director Busby Berkeley wherein she played the wide-eyed Broadway newcomer who falls in love with the buoyant tenor, who was usually Dick Powell.

Al, Erle and Al Junior

Erle:

Al Jolson marries Erle Galbraith on March 23, 1945.

"Oh, this is so silly. I'm not anybody!"

So said Erle Jolson Krasna, Al Jolson's fourth wife, upon being requested to sign autographs for Jolson fans at the United States Post Office Ceremony unveiling of an Al Jolson Postage Stamp at New York's Lincoln Center in 1994. She was the special guest.

"To us, you are," said Jan Hernstat, then Vice President of the International Al Jolson Society.

Erle Galbraith first met Al Jolson while he was on tour entertaining our wounded fighting men at Arkansas area hospitals. Some believe that Erle was Jolson's nurse when he was in the hospital. That was not true. She was an X-ray technician from Hot Springs, Arkansas, simply beautiful, and among the personnel assigned to sit on the floor in front of the wounded GI's in the auditorium while Jolson performed so they could keep an eye on them in case of an emergency. After the show, she quietly approached Jolson and asked for an autograph. "I was looking at her as I signed her slip of paper, but nobody introduced us."

At Jolson's following show in Texas, he could not stop thinking about her. He put a call through to the Colonel in charge of the earlier show in Hot Springs at five in the morning to ask the name of the girl who asked him for the autograph.

"I wrote to her the next day. I told her I believed she had the kind of face that would register in the movies and that I could get her a job in Hollywood."

Jolson was old enough to be her father, of course, so he would arrange for to stay with some married friends who would watch out for her. The Galbraith family sent an emissary to Jolson to say they rejected his offer as they were worried about her living alone in Hollywood. Jolson reassured him that it was a *bona fide* offer and that he had secured a job for her at Columbia Pictures through it's President, Harry Cohn. He said he was not in love with the girl and had no designs on her whatever.

"She arrived by train in a few days eight hours late," recalled Jolson," and I spent the last three hours sleeping on a bench waiting for her. This was also the day the doctors told me that I'd have to undergo an operation for removal of a lung."

So, there he was with an operation at hand and a protégé on his hands. Later, when Jolson was recuperating, Erle Galbraith came to the hospital to visit him.

"As she walked through the door I knew that I was head-over-heels in love with this girl and I felt like a kid of sixteen. And every time I saw her from then on, it got worse."

Convalescing in Palm Springs, Jolson sent a letter to Erle's father asking for his daughter's hand in marriage. A sizzling Special Delivery note came back quickly, stating: "You are old enough to be my daughter's father! I have never heard anything so insulting in all my born days."

Disappointed, Jolson read the letter to Erle. "I guess I'd better go home and talk to daddy," she told Jolson, "I can twirl my dad around my little finger." And she did. They were to be married on March 23, 1945, after his lengthy recovery.

"Well, we got married and we're all best of friends, and her mother is out of this world."

Jolson was sixty and Erle was twenty-two. They had a wonderful life together. They adopted a son and named him Asa Albert Jolson, Jr.

The marriage was to last a little over five years, until Jolson passed away in October, 1950, just after his strenuous three-week tour of Korea. Erle Jolson was just 28.

> Erle Jolson: "No matter where we are, Al is like a busman on a holiday-he can't get away from what's going on in the world of entertainment. It's his world. He lives it, breathes in it, would be miserable without it."

Jolson Society member Stan Gerloff once asked Erle Jolson if she had urged Jolson to retire during the Summer of 1950: "No..there wasn't anybody alive who could get him to do anything he didn't want to do. He would have never retired...it would have never entered his head. Even during World War II when people said he was retired, he really wasn't. He kept busy doing radio work or singing for the troops."

EPILOGUE:

In 1951 comedian Jack Benny introduced Erle to journalist, playwright, Norman Krasna, who had won the Academy Award for his 1943 screenplay

*Princess O'Rourke, and was currently a film producer
and RKO executive. Erle and Norman married and
later resided in Switzerland for twenty years. He
passed away in 1984, and was survived by Erle
and their three children Beth, Emily and David, and,
of course, Albert Jolson, Jr. Erle passed away in
January, 2004 in Century City, California. She was
eighty-one.*

The Jolsons (Ruby & Al) with theatrical producer Daniel Frohman. Al was
Elected Honorary Mayor of Encino, Dec. 1935.

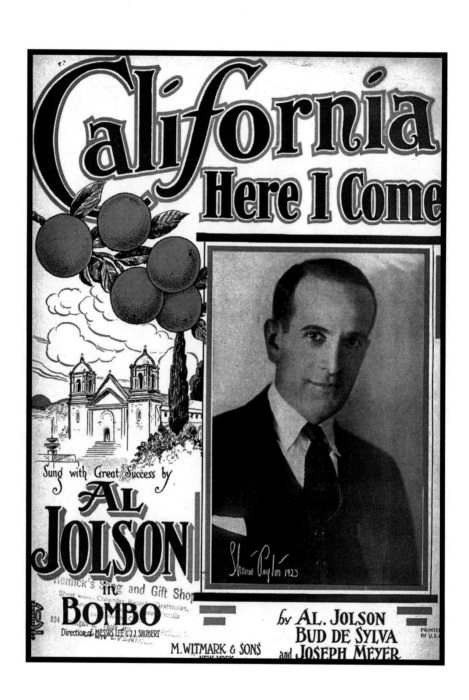

PART FOUR
TRIBUTES FROM FRIENDS

George and Gracie

Personal Glimpses
In Their Own Words

PATTY ANDREWS

Lead singer of the famed singing trio the Andrews Sisters, the three girls from Minneapolis who sang and recorded prolifically with her sisters Maxine and La Verne mostly during World War II with the songs "Boogie Woogie Bugle Boy," "Rumors Are Flying," "I'll Be With You in Apple Blossom Time," "Don't Sit Under the Apple Tree," and "Hold Tight," among many others including those with both Bing Crosby and Al Jolson.

From my interview with Patty in November of 2005 from her home in Northridge, California.

"We always enjoyed recording with Al Jolson. He was a show business great. He would always clown around when we were recording keeping us in a relaxed mood. During the sessions at Decca he would always be looking for

a laugh. Doing "Way Down Yonder in New Orleans" and "The Old Piano Roll Blues," Jolie would keep us laughing until the light went on to record. It really loosened us up and we sang with joy.

"On the *Kraft Music Hall* show in 1949 we sang with him as guest stars. Jolie was a cutup even then. We would do a comedy sketch with him as a parody of the song "Sonny Boy," which we also recorded. That recording enjoyed a bit of its own fame. Jolson loved having fun and he was a nice man with a big, big voice, and a big, big heart, and always made us girls feel comfortable."

CONNIE HAINES

Our Interview on July 15, 2005 from her home in Clearwater, Florida. Connie wasn't feeling good that day and was waiting for her doctor to pay her a house call to try to find the source of her dizzy spells. I had sent her a Wolferman's "Get Well" package of jams, fruits and English muffins and a case of her books, "Snootie Little Cutie," that we put together a few years earlier. Connie, of course, sang shoulder-to-shoulder with Frank Sinatra for three years when they both started singing in the band of Harry James, who discovered both talents at about the same time. Sinatra and Haines shifted to the Tommy Dorsey band, where, with the help of

Larry O'Brien (Current Glenn Miller Orchestra Director), Connie and Richard Grudens

Jo Stafford and the Modernaires, recorded a long list of tunes like "Let's Get Away from It All," and "Snootie Little Cutie."

"When Al Jolson appeared in his own show at the famed Hollywood Bowl in the early 1940s, when Frank Sinatra and I were singing stars with Tommy Dorsey, he arranged to have us available in the first row of seats and then, as a surprise, asked us to come up on stage with him where he introduced us to the vast, outdoor audience and said some very nice things. Frank and I sang our popular recording "Let's Get Away from It All" backed by the studio orchestra. It was the 1940s and we were very young and just beginning to catch on with the public recently singing with Tommy, after leaving Harry James' band. Later in the program we were thrilled to watch Jolson perform from backstage. Frank really enjoyed and revered Al Jolson. He, like Bing Crosby, held Al Jolson as one of his singing heroes. I remember Al Jolson being a warm and charming person. When he sang you felt the joy of his charisma and his strength from anywhere you were watching. I never heard anyone

Frank Sinatra and Connie Haines

sing like that before. I don't think anyone has ever equaled him. He didn't need a microphone. He just sang his heart out with great joy and was an inspiration to so many later performers. "

Frankie Laine and Richard Grudens

FRANKIE LAINE

My Interview with him September 2005:

Frankie Laine is one of the great singing performers. He lives in San Diego high up over the city in a charming home filled with memorabilia of his past performing history. At 94 (in March, 2006), his song catalog includes "Mule Train," "Jezebel," "That's My Desire," "High Noon," "I Believe," "Moonlight Gambler," "Rockin'Chair," "Cry of the Wild

Goose," and "That Lucky Old Sun," which is also the title of his 1993 autobiography, *Lucky Old Son*.

"I once skipped school to go downtown to the movies and see Al Jolson in *The Singing Fool*. It was my initial introduction to that master entertainer who was at the peak of his game. He electrified me. I watched him fall to his knees and sing "Sonny Boy." I knew then what I wanted to do with my life. I was so impressed that I sat through the movie twice until I knew the lyrics and the melody cold.

I rounded up the kids at home and into the bedroom for an impromptu performance of Al Jolson's 'Sonny Boy'. When my mother saw me, she demanded to know where I had learned such a tune, figuring I hadn't learned it at choir practice, where I was supposed to have been.

"Richard, she got so mad and smacked me when she learned I also skipped school. Anyway, as you can guess, I remained a loyal Jolson fan for life. Still am. The day I met him on the set of *Jolson Sings Again* at Columbia and stood for a photo with him, was one of the best days of my life. He was a warm, wonderful personality.

"I was told that when Jolson first heard my recording of "That's My Desire" on the radio, he called my friend, disc jockey Al Jarvis, to find out who was singing it. Al told him that it was his roommate, and Jolson said, "That guy is one of the best singers to come down the pike in a long while. He's going to put all of us old-timers out of business.

"Praise like that from the likes of Al Jolson meant the world to me. Many stories have been written since then that made Jolson out to be a cold and rude egotist who often snubbed fellow performers. I only know that the gentleman I met was gregarious, likable, and very kind to a young and struggling, up-and-coming singer."

JO STAFFORD

Vocalist and recording star with Tommy Dorsey's Orchestra who sang with Frank Sinatra, Connie Haines, and The Pied Pipers back in the 1940s. She was known as the Voice of Home and G.I. Jo to G.I.'s during World War II when she recorded the tunes "I'll Be Seeing You," "Embraceable You," and "There Are Such Things."

Jo Stafford

"Never say to me that Al Jolson isn't one to help a lady in distress. Just before I was to perform on his radio show, I realized I had forgotten the belt to my dress. I said to Jolson that I could not face an audience without my belt, that it would make the dress look funny. 'What'll I do?' I asked the great one. " "Here, kid," Jolson volunteered, "take mine!" Jolson had whipped off his belt from his trousers. "But," I stammered, "aren't you afraid - well, you know - that your pants will come down?"

"So what," Jolson replied, "after all, if Fred Allen can do it for a radio gag, why not Jolson?"

"The broadcast went off without a hitch or fallen pants."

EVELYN KEYES

Played the Ruby Keeler role in *The Jolson Story*, and was Suellen O'Hara in *Gone with the Wind* and costarred in *Here Comes Mr. Jordan:*

Jolie and Evelyn

"Al Jolson, to me, was amazing. He had energy to spare. He bounced around on stage and even when he wasn't on the stage or in front of the camera. As everyone knows, Al Jolson called himself the World's Greatest Entertainer, and I know why. His eyes danced and sparkled all the time. When he was in the recording studio- in a sound booth with headphones on - and with only one lung - he was sensational. In his presence, you knew all that was said about him was true. But, you had to be there."

JERRY LEWIS

The stupendous slapstick comedian half of Martin & Lewis, who with singer Dean Martin, entertained in night clubs all over, and later in films, and on television for many years, until they went their separate ways.

"The word for Jolson was stunning. There's been nobody like him since, and nobody before him. I remember my dad, also a performer, doing Jolson. And I listened, and I learned. And, now, as my tribute, in my one-man shows, I always do several Jolson songs. Whenever I do a concert, even in Spain, I do the Jolson songs, and the audience responds. Perhaps they know about Jolson, perhaps not, but they realize that he was a magnetic person. In October, 1950 I had played the Paramount in New York. I took a plane for an engagement in San Francisco. In Chicago, at the airport, I saw the headline: JOLSON DEAD! I cried most of the way out to San Francisco,"

TONY BENNETT

Tony Bennett and I had a long conversation about all the singers before him and that included Al Jolson. Tony is grateful for all his teachers, like Jolson who paved his way along with his many contemporaries. Tony Bennett keeps going and going, just like the Energizer Bunny.

"He was the father of Pop songs in our time, the pioneer who put just about every performer today in his debt. Al Jolson taught us the power of 'taking care of biz' when it comes to entertaining an audience. No one was like him. No one could do what he did for show business."

Richard and Tony Bennett

JERRY VALE

Wondrous Columbia recording star with fifty-two albums to his credit, Jerry Vale has entertained millions from New York's Copacabana to premiere venues in Las Vegas and has appeared in theater, films, festivals, television and radio right up to today.

"Like many of you, I too watched *The Jolson Story* a number of

Jerry Vale and Richard Grudens

times and was mesmerized over and over again. It helped point the way for me into this wonderful business of entertainment where he was undoubtedly the King. So Jolson is one of my favorites, and I'm certain, the champion of so many entertainers who followed him from the corridors of Tin Pan Alley to Broadway's Shubert Alley and beyond."

MICHAEL FEINSTEIN

Current, consummate cabaret performer and recording artist of mostly the great American songbook, who once catalogued the works of George and Ira Gershwin while working for Ira between 1977 and 1983, until Ira's passing:

"Jolson died six years before I was born, and yet remains one of the most vibrant and living figures I have ever encountered. When I first heard his voice, I was overwhelmed by the bravura and nerve and mournfulness, by the vaudevillian theatricality, and by the Jewishness of it.

"I believe that people respond to his songs and forgive the corny lyrics because of the memories they evoke. The Jolson persona is so resilient that almost any singer can up a Jolson medley in his or her act and know that it will work -and we almost all do some *Jolson*, including me."

Michael Feinstein

DAVID EVANIER

"What was it about Jolson? *The Jolson Story* and *Jolson Sings Again* changed the emotional landscape of my life. I lived, breathed Jolson; went to the Commodore Record Shop every week

for the newest Jolson record. Milt Gabler saw me coming and held out the record for me. When Jolson did the *Lux Radio Theater*, I was exploding with excitement. Radio station WVNJ was playing Jolson records the same night, so I started with WVNJ and milk and Oreo cookies and finally it was time for the real Jolie on *Lux*. What a night.

"When he died, I remember my father tiptoeing into my room while I was sleeping to tell me the news. He loved Jolson. Now I know that almost every little Jewish and

David Evanier

Italian boy felt the same way. We all wished we'd been alive when he sang at the Winter Garden. I auditioned for *Ted Mack's Amateur*

Hour miming to "Rosie You Are My Posie." This year I found out that Bobby Darin's manager, Steve Blauner, did the same thing. Sinatra, Darin, Jimmy Roselli, Tony Bennett adored Jolson, were mesmerized by him. You can hear Jolson in Roselli's "Rock a Bye" and "Give My Regards to Broadway," in Darin's "About a Quarter to Nine," He had scores of imitators, beginning with Georgie Jessel and Norman Brooks, a sure sign of greatness and originality.

"So what was it? The deep paternal voice, the strong father figure, the passion, the emotion. A totally unique voice, persona and incredible bravado. Whatever it was, it affected the lifetimes of millions."

David Evanier is the biographer of Jimmy Roselli, *Making the Wiseguys Weep*; Bobby Darin, *Roman Candle*; Joe Panatoliano - Who's Sorry Now? and the forthcoming authorized bio-discography of *Louis Prima*.

BILL FARRELL

My Philadelphia friend Anthony Di Florio III interviewed vocalist Bill Farrell about his one and only appearance before Al Jolson. Bill, from Cleveland, Ohio, was the regular singer on *The Bob Hope Show* in 1947, along with Doris Day, and traveled with Bob on the USO shows.

While appearing on the *Bob Hope Swan* radio show in 1948, I got to meet one of my idols, Al Jolson, who was a guest on the show. "It was a great thrill when I met Al Jolson.

"My father had Jolson records always playing in our house and I sang along with them. So, you could imagine how excited I was to work with Al Jolson."

When Bill was rehearsing on stage, Jolson came in with Harry Askt, Bill Farrell his piano accompanist, and a few others.

"I sang my usual four songs and put a special 'oomph' in my singing because I knew Jolson would be listening."

After his fourth song, Bill went down into the seats to meet Jolson. "I went up to him and said, 'Mr. Jolson, my father would be very proud of me today. You are his favorite, and mine, too!"

"Kid, you have a good voice," Jolson said with high praise, "I like the way you sing."

"Wow! You could have knocked me over with a feather," Bill Farrell said. It was a true adventure for this very young singer who never met him again, but never forgot that terrific day he shared the stage, and appeared on the same show with Al Jolson."

JOE FRANKLIN

KING OF NOSTALGIA

Back when Joe Franklin was seventeen, he worked as the music librarian and record picker for New York's legendary "Make Believe Ballroom" disc jockey Martin Block on radio station WNEW. That was back in the 1940s. Now, in 2005, some 60 odd years later, Joe has become an icon of his own.

Joe Franklin has been a long time admirer of Al Jolson having promoted him consistently on his shows and has provided personal information and photos for this guide to Jolson.

Joe F., Tony B. and Janet Cantor Gari at the Annual Long Island Jolson Festival, August 2005, *Madeline Grudens Photo*

He started in television in 1950, and is credited with pioneering the talk show format that has translated into a prolific art form spawning shows like the *Tonight Show*, *Dick Cavett*, *David Letterman*, *Conan O'Brien*, and the *Today Show* with all its counterparts. His show, simply called the Joe Franklin Show, was the longest running show in television when it dropped the curtain in 1990. It ran for 43 consecutive years.

Richard With Joe Franklin at the Jolson Conference,
August 27, 2005

But, by now, *The Tonight Show* has broken his record, but there were many more hosts. Joe was always alone as host. The Guinness Book of Records claims that Franklin holds the record for hosting 31,015 shows, and has been credited with helping to establish the careers of a number of popular show business personalities along the way.

"I did more than 28,000 episodes, interviewing everybody and anybody, which someone told me works out to about two episodes a day for over forty years."

Sure, Joe's show was sometimes corny, but according to Kathryn Crosby, it was mostly valid and featured great interviews helpful to hopefuls who needed exposure to help accelerate their career when no one else cared. Joe Franklin always cared, so everyone wanted to be on his show.

"Anyone in show business was welcome to appear on my show. Sammy Davis, Jr., Bill Cosby, Barry Manilow, Barbra

Streisand, and even Woody Allen got their jump-start on my show. My Bing Crosby interview, with his wife, Kathryn, is still the interview to beat. In Richard Grudens book *Bing Crosby-Crooner of the Century* the entire interview is printed exactly as we aired it. Read it and you get the whole story."

Over the years Joe Franklin has been a keen supporter of The International Al Jolson Society and is a Celebrity Honorary and winner of the 1993 coveted *Irvin Warwick Award*, an elevation to the highest honor the Society can bestow.

Known to one and all as the King of Nostalgia, Schtick and Patter; the last of the organic show hosts, Joe Franklin boasts that he has interviewed some 300,000 guests over the years. Whew! Joe wrote a book about the many standup comics he has known and calls it *Joe Franklin's Encyclopedia of Comedians.* Joe has appeared as himself in a number of movies including Woody Allen's *Broadway Danny Rose* and *Ghost Busters*.

Joe has also hosted a special series called *When Movies Were Movies* featuring old movies interspersed with his own trivia that began back in 1980 on New York's Channel 9. And Joe was the host of a weekly radio program, called *Memory Lane*, on WOR AM Radio in New York on Saturday nights during the 1990s. Joe Franklin's Comedy Club is located in Charley O's Bar and Grill, 713 Eighth Avenue.

In 1995, Joe launched a series of nostalgic CDs on Sony's Legacy Imprint with titles "*Growing Up with Radio*," "*The Roaring Twenties Again*," and "*Hoo-Ray for Hollywood*," each featuring a dozen selections of mostly unreleased original material on compact disc, each accompanied by a nostalgic Franklin monologue. In 2002, International Al Jolson Society member Brian Decker interviewed Joe Franklin about their mutual idol, Al Jolson:

"When I was picking records for the great Martin Block on the Make Believe Ballroom show Jolson came in and Martin asked me to bring in a Jolson record, so I brought in Jolson's 1912 recording of "Movin' Man, Don't Take My Baby Grand," and Martin played it while Jolson looked back and told me to: 'Break that record, Franklin,' while the record was playing on the air.

"I enjoyed and prefer the earlier Jolson voice. People say that Jolson's voice was different when he made *The Jolson Story*. And it was! So was Crosby's voice different over six different decades, and you can say Sinatra had six different voices, too. Jolson's voice became deeper, raspier, just different in 1946, after he had his left lung removed in 1945. That made the difference.

"I enjoyed Jolson's earlier material, like "Hello Central, Give Me No Man's Land," which still gives people goose-pimples when they hear it. And I enjoy "On the Road to Calais," another of the Brunswick recordings. "Mother of Mine (I Still Have You.)" is another favorite. But, when he did "Alexander's Ragtime Band" with Bing, that, along with his duets with Patty, Maxine, and Laverne, the wonderful Andrews Sisters, were all great recordings that will live on. He had a good time making them.

"You see, Brian, all you needed for a successful show in those days was the name of Al Jolson on the marquee. His name appeared a lot on sheet music, something both he and the songwriters needed for success, even though he probably never wrote a line or a note. His name on the sheet music was music to everyone's ears and just about guaranteed the song's success."

Stop in to visit legendary Joe Franklin at his restaurant, or tune in to his radio show on weekends. He will be glad to see you or know you are still listening.

SYBIL JASON

In 2005, one of the most popular child stars of the Golden Age of Hollywood, Sybil Jason, had her memoirs published highlighting her career in the movies and beyond. She calls it *My Fifteen Minutes*. When Sybil co-starred with Al Jolson in *The Singing Kid*, she stole a few charming scenes that endeared her to millions, not unlike her counterpart Shirley Temple.

To Richard: I really adored Jolie! Blessings, Sybil - From the Singing Kid

Recently Sybil told me she absolutely loved and respected her co-star, Al Jolson.

> "From the time I was a little kid, I remember my father singing Al Jolson songs to me in my crib. I never dreamed that one day I would be in Hollywood, far from my home in South Africa, co-starring in the movies with this great performer whom my father loved."

After making that movie, Sybil maintained an ongoing relationship with Al Jolson and his wife Ruby Keeler. All three appeared together in a two-reel movie short *A Day at Santa Anita*. Before appearing in *The Singing Kid* Sybil had already completed *Little Big Shot* in which she starred with '30s character Edward Everett Horton. When she heard she would be starring in a movie with Al Jolson, her memory bank received a jolt:

"Here was my father's magical hero and I working together. I would have loved to see the look on my father's face when my parents received our cablegram informing them."

Insofar as Sybil's remembering her experiences with Mr. Jolson, they are remembered as through the eyes of child.

"Of course, we both had to go through preproduction and also had to learn and rehearse the songs. Harold Arlen and E.Y. 'Yip' Harburg, who had composed the songs for the Judy Garland classic movie *The Wizard of Oz,* also wrote our songs for *The Singing Kid.*

"They gave me the script and the words and music to "You're the Cure for What Ails Me," which was the song I would share in a duet with Mr. Jolson. I studied my lines and rehearsed the song with a piano which I did at the studio. There were breaks in the song where others came in so I had to get used to that.

WARNER BROS PRESENT
LITTLE BIG SHOT
WITH
SYBIL JASON • ROBERT ARMSTRONG
GLENDA FARRELL • EDW. EVERETT HORTON

"When Mr. Jolson spotted me in the studio one afternoon during rehearsal, he immediately shouted across the room to me saying, 'Sybilla, come over here and meet your Uncle Al.'" Jolson gave Sybil a big hug, then looked into her eyes and with a big grin on his face said 'You gonna do just fine, baby,' and then kissed the top of her head. He stood up and said to her, 'You wanna sing a song with me?'

"Well, we began rehearsal. I adored him on sight and there

were absolutely no problems connected with our duet..no key changes...no rhythm changes...nothing. In fact, after rehearsal, Mr. Jolson stepped over to my guardian and said he was amazed that I had such perfect timing for such a young child and that he got a big kick out of how I picked up on some of his facial expressions."
On the set, Sybil had begun to have continuing bouts of stomach aches that she brought to the attention of Jolson while they were waiting for a scene to be taken. Jolson dispatched her to the studio doctor whose office was really just a first-aid station. The doctor thought it perhaps was a symptom of appendicitis or simply a stomach spasm, which, for the moment, it was considered to be. "However, two days after the film was completed, I was rushed with severe pain to the hospital and had my appendix removed.

Sybil and Guy Kibbee

Al Jolson filled my hospital room with gifts and flowers and called me daily to check my progress. The nurses were thrilled when he called with that distinctive voice they easily recognized."

When Jolson discovered Sybil had a birthday while on the set, which was out on location some miles away, he presented her with a beautiful bicycle, complimenting her on her talent and work habits to everyone present and said how badly he felt that they were on location where she couldn't properly celebrate: "Baby," Jolson said, "I hope this makes up for it jus'a liddle bit." Everyone on the set was applauding, whistling while the photographers snapped photos.

Sybil never stopped riding around the location grounds on her new bike until it was time for dinner.

"I went to bed that night a very contented child. And as if the bike weren't enough, Jolie, as I called him, had catered a whole birthday party for this little kid and there were more presents to open."

Jolson always had an entourage of friends with him and Sybil remembers they were all very nice, but, reflecting later, thought they all looked like characters straight out of Damon Runyon's *Guys and Dolls*.

"I remember they wore party hats with lollipops in their mouths and sang a very loud and exuberant rendition of "Happy Birthday" to me. It was the most memorable birthday party I ever remember as a child."

Sybil caught up with Al Jolson sometime later at the Warner Ball in the Biltmore Hotel on April 23, 1937. More than one thousand stars, directors and producers attended that magnificent affair. They wrote a featured act for Sybil and Al that had them segue into their famous tune "You're the Cure for What Ails Me," the popular duet they had performed in *The Singing Kid*.

"Oh, Boy! We received a round of thunderous applause and a standing ovation. Jolie hugged me and whispered, 'We gottem, baby!' He was simply wonderful."

Later on, at the Shrine Auditorium, Sybil joined Al Jolson at a benefit where they did not perform together, but joined hands for a final bow at the end of the program. Later, attending a barbecue at the home of Al and Ruby, they supplied games, dolls, crayons and coloring books for Sybil and another youngster. Sybil remembered that she enjoyed the great variety of foods the Jolson's supplied that afternoon.

"It was many years before I saw Mr. Jolson again. I attended a live radio broadcast of the *Lux Radio Theater* where he played himself in a radio version of the movie *Jolson Sings Again*. I went backstage to try to see him. The attendant was reluctant, but, after some urging went to Jolson whereupon he asked to have me escorted to his dressing room. A sense of panic gripped me for a moment as I did not know what kind of reception I would encounter after so many years. When the door of the dressing room opened, it was 1936 all over again. He gave me a big bear hug and made me comfortable and wanted to know everything about my life since we last saw one another."

Jolson encouraged her to keep going if she wanted to continue a life in show business, as tough as it was for her at the time, and cited his own personal recall into show business after his own hiatus, being ignored by producers: "Baby, don't lettum get t'ya. Just a short time ago, Jolie couldn't even get a spot on a benefit show - but look at me now. I outlasted 'em all."

"I'll never forget his words to me that day."

In reality, Jolson had only five months to live from that meeting with Sybil Jason. For many years thereafter the International Al Jolson Society has flown Sybil to appear as their guest at reunions held all over the country where she would relate her favorite Al Jolson stories and share with members her rare 16 mm home movies that were taken while on location during the filming of *The Singing Kid*.

On September 9. 1994, Sybil had the honor of unveiling the Al Jolson Commemorative Postage Stamp on the first day of issue in Los Angeles, California, and again, on October 14, 2000 in Palm Springs, to help unveil Al Jolson's star on the *Sidewalk of Stars* placed right in front of the historic Plaza Theater where Jolson once had regularly appeared.

On October 26, 2000, in Pasadena, California, Sybil attended the opening night of a musical called *Jolson*, where she met Al's wife Erle for the first time face-to-face, although they had previously spoke to one another by phone:
"Erle Jolson was one of the nicest and warmest ladies I have ever met. We talked and shared stories about her wonderful husband amidst lots of laughing and some crying."

On a final note from Sybil Jason: "For those who would still prefer to think of Al Jolson as a selfish and egotistical man, I much prefer to remember him as a kind, generous man with one big gargantuan talent."

Anthony Drake, Tony B., and Sybil Jason

Sybil Jason recently lost her own dear husband, Anthony Drake. "He was the love of my life. We were married fifty-seven happy years, Richard."

Sybil has, for the moment, decided to retire and live quietly with her daughter, Toni.

I've got a feeling she'll be back soon.

FILMS OF SYBIL JASON:

Barnacle Bill - 1935
Dance Band - 1935
Little Big Shot - 1935
A Dream Comes True - 1935
I Found Stella Parish - 1935
The Singing Kid - 1936
The Changing of the Guard - 1936

The Captain's Kid - 1936
A Day at Santa Anita - 1937
The Great O'Malley - 1937
Little Pioneer - 1937
The Little Diplomat - 1937
Comet Over Broadway - 1938
Woman Doctor - 1939
The Little Princess - 1939
The Blue Bird - 1940

DAVEY LEE

AL JOLSON: "He's only three---but the kid's a born actor!

"We had to have a kid to play Sonny Boy in *The Singing Fool*. The casting director looked at one hundred-and-eighty kids ---

and was still looking. We had to have somebody --- and get him quick.

"I was hurrying to the studio one morning when I noticed a youngster playing around on the grass plot in front. I stopped and asked him what he was up to. He said he was going to play. Something about that kid got me. I squatted down beside him and asked his name.

"'Davey Lee,' he said. 'Are you an actor?'
"I admitted it. 'A good actor?' said the kid.

Davey Lee

"That made me laugh. He laughed too---and threw his arms around my neck and asked me for a ride.

"That settled it. I knew I had found Sonny Boy.

"I was so sold on the kid for the part that I agreed to take all the responsibility. He had never been in a picture before. Frankly,

I was a little nervous about him when we got going. But, I trusted my hunch and taught him his lines and how to wait for his cue. "He worked out really well, so I knew he didn't have to be watched so closely. He always remembered the words I had told him to wait for, and he waited."

Jolson was certain Davey Lee had a great future. "Warner Brothers signed him to make a picture with Rin Tin Tin, the famous acting dog. I'm mighty proud of discovering Davey lee. I feel just like Columbus,"

Born in Hollywood on December 29, 1924, Davey Lee celebrated his 80th birthday in a nursing home, the Windsor Gardens in Hollywood. Davey Lee was the first child star of the talkies and starred with Al Jolson in *The Singing Fool* in 1928 at a mere four year's old. *The Singing Fool* held the record as box office champ in Hollywood until it was unseated by no less than the masterpiece *Gone With the Wind* in 1938.

I spoke briefly to Davey Lee in August 2005, but it was tough for him to talk or recall much because of his medical condition, so we kept it brief.

In that famous, extemporaneous, 4AM Barry Gray WOR radio interview in New York in 1947, Jolson spoke of meeting up

once again with Davey Lee while he was on tour in early 1950 for the USO entertaining the troops. Davey Lee, then a well decorated serviceman with Uncle Sam, approached Jolson and asked if he remembered him playing in *The Singing Fool* and sitting on his lap while Jolson sang "Sonny Boy?" When Jolson realized it was Davey Lee, he gave him the usual, enthusiastic bear hug and reminisced joyously about their time together making movies.

DAVEY LEE MADE SIX MOVIES AS A CHILD STAR.

The Squealer in 1930
Skin Deep in 1929
Say It with Songs in 1929
Frozen River in 1929
Sonny Boy in 1929
The Singing Fool in 1928

BEVERLY ROBERTS

THE JOLSON CONNECTION

Beverly, Sybil and Jolson - *The Singing Kid*

It is 2005, and Beverly Roberts is ninety-one years old and spry as a kitten. Our telephone conversation was quickly interrupted because she had been cooking when I called her and had to excuse herself, so we continued the following evening.

Beverly is truly an elegant lady of film, radio, television, and the stage. She has been performing her craft since the 1930s. She has done it all and for a long time. She was born in 1914 in Brooklyn, New York.

Her association with Jolson began with her first film, *The Singing Kid*, where she appeared as Al's love interest, Ruth Haines, and as the mother of Sybil Haines, played by the charming child star, Sybil Jason. Beverly explained that she, of course, knew of Al Jolson, but was not a fan of his early stage works having never seen him before the film went into production. *The Singing Kid*, Al's last starring film for Warner Brothers, was released in 1936.

Beverly's believable performance was constrained by it appearing late in the film, although it remained an important role. I enjoyed her simplicity and shyness as a contrast to Jolson's eagerness and drive in his respective role. Beverly maintained her friendship with Sybil Jason right up to today.

Beverly had quite a nice career since that first effort.

She regularly portrayed assertive women in get-tough movies, playing characters that ran a lumber camp to one operating a fleet of buses or running a medical mission.

Her acting education at Eva La Gallienne's Civic Repertory Theater Company endeared her to stage-acting. But, that changed when she was spotted singing in a New York City nightclub by a Warner Brothers talent scout. Her first role was with Jolson. Other roles followed when she appeared with a young Humphrey Bogart in *One Fatal Hour*.

The film *China Clipper* teamed her with Pat O'Brien in 1936, and in Warner Brothers first Technicolor production, Beverly starred in her most prestigious film, *God's Country and the Woman*. It was filmed on location at the foot of Mt. St. Helens.

After a batch of film productions, Beverly returned to her first love, live performances on stage singing and acting. By the late 1940s, and through the early '50s, she performed in a great number of radio and television programs.

Margaret and Al Jolson

Beverly: "In my time, when an actress reached 30 and passed that so-called sexually desired age, that was it, unless you were Joan Crawford or Greta Garbo. Older women have more opportunities now."

1954 found her as the administrator of the Theater Authority, representing the five entertainment unions that exercised jurisdiction over the appearance of performers at charity events. Beverly retired in 1977 to Laguna Niguel, California, where she still resides. In March 2002, she was honored at the Del Mar Theater in Santa Cruz, California, when the film *China Clipper* was shown at its grand reopening.

"The star of that film was really the *China Clipper* itself, overshadowing any of us actors at the time, " Beverly said. Beverly enjoyed television acting. She appeared in *Kraft Television Theater* productions and in *Robert Montgomery Presents* to excellent reviews.

MARGARET WHITING

VOCALIST AND DAUGHTER OF COMPOSER RICHARD WHITING

"When I got the offer, I jumped for joy," Margaret said. "We were to perform for the radio version of *Alexander's Ragtime Band*. The movie had featured Tyrone Power, Alice Faye, Don Ameche, and Broadway star Ethel Merman."

Margaret Whiting and I go back to the 1980s when I first interviewed her for a *Make Believe Ballroom* show at the Westbury Music Fair on Long Island. We have maintained our friendship over the years and lastly at the Bing Crosby 2002 conference at Hofstra University. WNEW disc-jockey great William B. Williams was the emcee who had invited me to do a story on the staged version of the popular radio show that featured Billy Eckstine, Margaret Whiting, and the Glenn Miller Orchestra, under the direction of Larry O'Brien, who directs, to this day, the great Glenn

Margaret Whiting and Richard Grudens

Miller Orchestra.

Years before, in the 1940s, when young vocalist Margaret Whiting began her regular appearances on the *Eddie Cantor Radio Show*, she was invited to appear on the prestigious *Lux Radio Theater*, which, at the time, was a prime-time dramatic radio show that showcased movies in abridged form. The show's narrator was the one and only legendary film director Cecil B. De Mille.

For the radio version, Dinah Shore was to repeat Alice Faye's role, and Margaret was to perform Merman's part.

"Her part had the best songs and was the girl who loved the guy but couldn't get him. I thought that was just great. The extra added attraction was that Al Jolson was going to make one of his rare appearances. Of course, when he came in everyone practically genuflected to him, including George Gruskin. George had intimated that since his client Dinah Shore was the bigger name, she should be given preferential treatment. That did not sit well with me. But I smiled and we started rehearsal. George was sitting in the control booth, and we lowly actors were sitting around waiting for our calls. The director said to Jolson;

'How would you like to proceed with the musical numbers, Mr. Jolson?'

"Jolson said, putting his arm around me, 'Well, I think we should start with Margaret here. After all, I've known her folks all these years, and I feel I have to take care of her.'

According to Margaret: "I was overjoyed as *Alexander's Ragtime Band* turned out to be one of the great shows done on radio, thanks in part to the appearance of the great Al Jolson."

Margaret Whiting also appeared on radio with Al Jolson in 1949 on the April 14th *Kraft Music Hall* and sang a duet with Al entitled "Ain't We Got Fun?"

RUDY WISSLER

The efforts of Rudy Wissler is one of *The Jolson Story*

secrets that we are pleased to feature in this book. Millions have seen *The Jolson Story* biography. Few knew that Rudy Wissler sang his heart out, too, in this supremely entertaining film. While Scotty Beckett neatly portrayed the young acting Jolson, it was Rudy's sweet voice that carried each tune forward.

Rudy Wissler

In an interview with Jolson authority Ed Greenbaum, Rudy recounted his contribution to The Jolson Story.

Since *The Jolson Story,* Rudy has appeared in a number of notable films and stage performances. In films it was *Tomorrow the World, Boys Ranch, Nancy Goes to Rio, The Human Comedy, Jack London,* and *Cover Girl.* On stage it was Rodgers and Hammersteins's *Flower Drum Song, Annie,* and *The Music Man.* He has also appeared on many radio and television programs including appearances on *Arthur Godfrey,* and the *Edgar Bergen-Charlie McCarthy Show.*

> **Ed Greenbaum: "But, it was Rudy's**
> **sterling work in The Jolson Story that interests**
> **Jolson fans. There, he provided the beautiful**
> **singing voice for young Asa Yoelson."**

"The combination of his endearing voice and Scotty Beckett's near perfect lip-syncing to some of the turn-of-the-century's finest songs made an unforgettable impression on the audience and contributed, in a large way, to the film's great success."

Ed began by asking Rudy about his assignment on the film. Rudy explained that the Jolson film was nothing unusual for him to do at that time, since he was an employee of Columbia Pictures and this was part of his job. Rudy had known Scotty Beckett as a friend, but they never got together during the filming or recording session.

Ed: "He recalled the first time he met Jolson. Musical director Morris Stoloff and arranger Saul Chaplin introduced Rudy to Jolson as the boy who was going to sing the part of young Asa. Apparently, Jolson did not understand why Rudy wasn't going to be cast in the film. The studio reasoning was that Beckett looked more like Larry Parks. Jolson wanted Rudy to appear in the movie and convinced the director to try to apply makeup to achieve the needed likeness. The fact that Rudy's nose was not, as Rudy put it: '...as beautiful as Larry Parks' nose,' concluded that even Jolson had to admit it would not work, thereby excluding Rudy from the acting role."

Rudy's remembrance of Jolson was quite clear: "Al's demeanor was professional and tolerant. He was an intelligent man, and knew this biographical film was going to work to his advantage. He expected the best product from everyone involved in the film. There was no temper, no nonsense, or no distractions ever, from Jolson."

According to Ed Greenbaum, there were two songs Rudy recorded that were never included in the film, "Every Little Movement Has a Meaning All It's Own," which was cut, and "Wait 'til the Sun Shines, Nellie," that was heard only in film promotions. Rudy Wissler recalled that after each recorded take, there was an immediate playback. By listening to each take over studio speakers, it was determined if another would be needed.

Rudy recalled that Jolson had all activity on *The Jolson Story* set interrupted for a while each afternoon while he dashed to his dressing room for the racing results on his radio. Obviously, Jolson loved the sport and was a first-rate horse racing spectator and gentleman gambler.

Rudy also said that once or twice during the recording session Jolson would hum along quite loudly, spoiling the take, only to be admonished and requested by the musical directors to be quiet.

Ed Greenbaum: "Rudy said he remembered with fondness working with Cantor Saul Silverman on the "Jewish hymn Ahavas Olom." He said it was the favorite number he performed for the film." Ed Greenbaum crossed his fingers when he asked Rudy if there had been surviving photographs taken at the recording sessions, especially with him and Jolson.

"No, but how I wished there had been," Rudy said. Still active in singing, Rudy Wissler has completed a new CD entitled "Rudy: A Musical Anthology - Or Life After Asa," that includes some newly-recorded, but old, sentimental chestnuts.

On June 21, 2006 Rudy Wissler will celebrate his 78th birthday.

From The Past

EDDIE CANTOR

Legendary Vaudeville and radio star who blessed us with his popular radio show and films singing signature songs "Making Whoopie," "Ida, Sweet as Apple Cider," and "If You Knew Suzie Like I Know Suzie," talking about the Jolson Sunday Night Specials at the Winter Garden.

"Oh, there were some other people occasionally on the stage: a line of dancing girls, enough of a company to keep things going while Jolie took a glass of water or mopped his brow off stage. But he was the show, and many the night he'd look at the audience about a quarter of eleven and say,'The girls are waiting backstage and they have some songs and dances, but they've worked pretty hard tonight, let's let them go home, huh? I'll stay here as long as you want, but let the poor kids go home, huh? And he'd send everybody home wile he stood there maybe another hour, singing, clowning, giving the audience the time of its life - and having the time of his own.

"Even after *The Jolson Story*, which was in 1947, he was still insecure. We were neighbors in Palm Springs. We walked together, talked together, ate together, and I knew him better than I had ever known him through the years. What amazed me was that this great personality had never learned how to live. He couldn't, there was something chemically wrong. The minute the curtain rang down, he died."

FRED ALLEN

Vaudeville and Radio Comedian of the thirties and forties, famous for his radio partners and his fued (fake) with Jack Benny.

"When Shubert units were in New York, many of the acts, including Al Jolson, made additional money playing Sunday Concerts. The Shuberts booked those concerts into their theaters that housed musical or dramatic shows during the week. One Sunday night I was booked into the theater where Al Jolson was appearing during the week

Fred Allen and Portland Hoffa

in his show Bombo. When I told one of my jokes, the musicians in the pit groaned. When I asked them about this unfavorable reaction, they told me that Al Jolson was telling the same joke in his show. The joke was ' The man is so deceitful he puts salt on his toupee to make people think he has dandruff.'"I knew I had originated the line. I wrote Mr. Jolson a letter and received this reply:"

AL JOLSON

October 13, 1921
Mr. Fred Allen
1493 Broadway
New York City

Mr. Dear Sir:

   I have your letter of the 11th regarding the "toupee" gag. In reply I beg to say that I have been using the same for the past three years. I have no desire to use anyone's material and would gladly give it up to save you any embarrassment of being accused of taking my material, but on the point of it being yours exclusively, I think that is open for argument.

As one N.V.A. to another I send you greetings along with the "toupee" gag.

Yours truly,
Al Jolson

"Al Jolson must have dictated this letter. He couldn't have read it because he continued to use the 'toupee' joke in his show for the rest of the season. Twenty years later, I met Al Jolson at the Hillcrest Golf Club in Beverly Hills. He told me that he used to see my act frequently and helped himself to my jokes. I thought the admission was flattering, but a mite delayed."

BOB HOPE

Everybody knows Bob Hope, total subject of my biography *The Spirit of Bob Hope*: "I don't know how long Al's been in show business, but when he got started, Sid Grauman (of Grauman's famed Chinese Theater) had him put his knee print in Plymouth Rock! Al and I both got our starts in vaudeville. My routine

Bob Hope and Richard Grudens

was a little different. I didn't sing 'Mammy' - I cried *Uncle*! There's a little bit of Jolson in all of us. Many a G.I. will remember the Jolson magnetism as he followed the men in service. Wherever the going was tough, yessir, in peace and in war, Al has been one of our most inspiring entertainers for as long as I can remember."

MARY MARTIN

Broadway star of both two leading Rodgers and Hammerstein blockbuster musical plays, *Sound of Music* and *South Pacific*.

"When I saw the first talkie where Jolson sang "Mammy", I cried for three weeks. Even now if I hear that song, I cry."

Mary Martin

GEORGE JESSEL

A Jolson contemporary-fellow artist, star of the stage show *The Jazz Singer*, and candidate for the movie role, which he turned down, or was turned down because of his demands:

George Jessel

"I had known Jolie for many years, ever since our first meeting in San Francisco with Eddie Cantor. Jolie, I will say here and now (1975) was truly one of the greatest entertainers America has ever produced. But offstage he was completely different.

I honestly lamented the passing of this great, great dynamic personality and talent and his impact on the theater. During the eulogy of Jolie I never ventured much about the man himself. For Jolie, too, like most men of extraordinary ability, was a man with many idiosyncrasies, and nobody got under his skin.

"He was only content while singing and acknowledging

applause; the rest of the time he was champing at the bit while getting ready to go - and if he was not on, he was disconsolate...He was cruel most times....But, God, what a great artist he was! However, egocentric is too small a word for Jolson. Nature had somehow contrived him to be particularly immune to anyone else's pains and problems, so that he was only affected by what was happening to him at any particular time.

"The word failure in connection with anything he had to do was something he never uttered. At a horse race, in the stock market, at the ball game, you would always hear Jolie had a winner, even if you knew he hadn't.

"Right after the stock market crash, when I was wiped out of $400,000, I met with Al again. Cantor had also lost a bundle and almost every one of our friends had gone broke. "I was lucky,' said Al, 'not commiserating with us at all, 'I sold everything the day before the crash.'"

JACK BENNY

Legendary comedian, film and television star whom most other comedians measure themselves by.

Mary Livingstone Benny:

"Our shows sometimes originated from Palm Springs Legion Hall. One week we were having Al Jolson as our guest star. Jolson was the only star I was in awe of...

Jack Benny and Ed Sullivan

"At the last rehearsal, we were running two minutes long. I explained to Jack and he suggested I ask Al Jolson to cut one of his songs.

"I looked at him and said, Jack, it's your show...why don't you ask him.?

"He smiled and said, "Not me, you're the producer. You talk to him." Yes, I was the show's producer and Jack was also in awe of Jolson. He loved Al. He said, "Now, go ahead and do your job." "Suddenly, I became the big man. Jack wasn't going to budge-so I went to find Al.

"Mr. Jolson, I began..."

"Please, I've told you before, call me Al..."

"Well Al, I said, we're two minutes over and....
He interrupted me saying, 'Then I'll cut one of my songs,' he volunteered. It was like taking one of the Psalms out of the Bible. 'Listen,' Al went on, 'maybe we'd better plan to cut a chorus from my second number, too...'

"Jolson was marvelous on the show, and it went off without a hitch. A few days later I finally saw Al Jolson appear in blackface singing 'Mammy,' 'Swanee,' and 'Waiting for the Robert E. Lee' at the Shrine Auditorium in Los Angeles for a benefit performance. Jack and I loved Al Jolson. We had a sincere admiration for him and he knew it. Jack and I had tears streaming down our face when Al Jolson sang his great songs. It was a moment I'll never forget..."

WILL ROGERS

Stage monologist and popular entertainer during Jolson's reign. Rogers died in an airplane crash with Pilot Wiley Post.

"The loss of old vaudeville was more than just

Will Rogers

the loss of seeing the show. Taking away vaudeville was just like taking the high school away, and wanting the pupil to jump from grammar school to college. Then, too, too many actors made the mistake of playing just on Broadway. They not only wore themselves out there, but they meant nothing on the road. No one knew them. That's how Jolson became so popular in the old days. Al was smart. He would always duck out of New York and play everywhere he could. He played many a one nighter in the very height of his tremendous popularity. He would draw anywhere. "

DANNY THOMAS

Danny Thomas

Legendary star of films and television, especially in *Make Room for Daddy* and star of the remake of *The Jazz Singer*. "In my opinion, Jolson was one of the finest entertainers of all time. The instant he stepped out on a stage, there was electricity in the air. You knew something terribly exciting was going to happen, and it usually did. No one could raise an audience to a fever pitch the way Jolson did, just by singing a song or chatting up the crowd."

LARRY PARKS

BY JAN HOLLY

PERSPECTIVE FROM A FAN

Jan Holly was born in England and was

truly a Stage Door Girl mostly at the famous London Palladium, a half-hour underground ride from her home, where she and her friends could see their musical heroes perform. As a kid she would reach into the fireplace and grab a handful of soot, blacken her face and treat the family to a Jolson evening of song. She wound up singing country music, which took her over the world entertaining U.S. Forces overseas, then moved permanently to the United States. Jan maintains a Larry Parks/Betty Garrett website for his fans to visit and enjoy.

"The Astoria Theater was a small town cinema in my home town of Seven Kings, Essex, England, where my dad would take me on Saturday afternoons. It's where I fell in love with Larry Parks, the actor who introduced Al Jolson to a whole new generation of fans when he portrayed the great singer in the films *The Jolson Story* and *Jolson Sings Again*, lip-syncing Jolson's songs so perfectly.

> ***Larry Parks***: "Stepping into Jolson's shoes was, for me, a matter of endless study, observation, energetic concentration to obtain, perfectly if possible, a simulation of the kind of man he was. It is not surprising, therefore, that while making The Jolson Story I spent 107 days before the camera and lost 18 pounds in weight."

"I never wanted to leave the cinema. I drove my friends crazy reenacting the entire Jolson movie for them over and over. I went back to see the film many times with my friends, sometimes skipping school, and even winding up in detention for talking about the movie during class.

"My hero, Larry Parks, was born Sam Klusman Parks on December 13, 1914 in Olathe, Kansas. While just a baby the family moved to Joliet, Illinois, where he grew up. He attended Farragut grammar school and played football for Joliet Township high school and went on to the University of Illinois with intentions of becoming a physician. Instead, he got his first taste of campus dramatics, and the world lost a doctor.

"Upon graduation he landed a job with a touring stock company and went on the road for thirty-five dollars a week and never looked back. At twenty-three, Larry went to New York and studied drama while working as a Radio City Tour Guide for $1.50 an hour.

Parks as Jolson

"When his dad passed away Larry returned home to help his mother at the family advertising agency. But, his heart wasn't in it, and when his friend, actor John Garfield, called offering him a part in a movie, he took off for Hollywood, only to discover the production had been canceled.

"Undaunted, and following a lucky test at Columbia Studios, Larry was signed and appeared in over thirty "B" films, including *Sing for Your Supper*, *Mystery Ship*, and *Harmon of Michigan*. Some of these were pretty good, some weren't. The film *She's a Sweetheart*, in which Larry plays the lead, is my favorite Larry Parks "B" film, but, of course, *The Jolson Story*, is his best and my all-time favorite.

"According to Larry, the highlight of his life was meeting and marrying the love of his life, Betty Garrett, who was active on Broadway at the time in the show *Call Me Mister*. The first three years of their marriage was spent commuting from Hollywood to New York and back again. Nevertheless, they remained happily married for thirty-one years and had two boys, Garrett, a musician, and Andrews, also an actor.

"In 1945, Larry won critical acclaim for his role in *Counterattack* with the great Paul Muni, making the studio bosses take notice and then choosing him for the lead in *Renegades*, with Evelyn Keyes, who later played the role of Julie Benson in *The Jolson Story*.

"Things were looking up for Larry, except that fellow actor Cornell Wilde and Larry were tested for the same roles and Wilde kept winning.

"When Columbia tested for *The Jolson Story*, he told Betty, "If Cornell is up for this role too, I may as well stay home." Larry Parks won the role of Al Jolson that would make him an international star. Now the hard work for him had really begun. Larry's perfectionist personality paid off as he was able to accurately lip-sync Jolson's voice and mime Jolson's actions. He practiced night and day singing to Al Jolson's' recordings and watching his old films until he caught the essence of the man. The movie was, of course, tremendously successful."

Larry Parks: "Al Jolson represented an age, an era, a tradition in show business that few can carry on."

"*The Jolson Story's* success led to the sequel *Jolson Sings Again*, also a remarkable success, with Larry Parks once again in the starring role of the World's Greatest Entertainer. Although he had a spat with the studios between the Jolson films, Larry took some time off to indulge in his hobbies of motorcycling and riding horses. The dispute resolved, he went to work on *Jolson Sings Again*, costarring Barbara Hale.

Larry and Betty

"Voted 'Bobbysoxers Man of the Year' in 1947, Larry Parks went on to star in *The Swordsman* with Ellen Drew. Ironically, Cornell Wilde directed Larry in the fencing scenes. I love this movie. Larry Parks shines in this role as much as he did in the Jolson bio's. Next came the films *Down to Earth* with Rita Hayworth followed by *The Gallant Blade* with Marguerite Chapman.

"The film *Love is Better Than Ever* with Elizabeth Taylor, and *Tiger By the Tale* with Constance Smith, was followed up with three years appearing in the stage production *Teahouse of the August Moon*. It is said that actor Marlon Brando was coached by Larry for his role in the film version.

"I was fortunate enough to finally see Larry and Betty in person at the London Palladium when they toured the English provinces in 1954, as they had done two years before. Larry later appeared with Montgomery Clift in the film *Freud* and continued acting on television and the stage until he passed away in 1975. To me Larry Parks was the ultimate brown-eyed, handsome man, and an excellent actor. I'll never tire of watching him on the screen over and over."

Author's Note: Betty Garrett and Larry Parks appeared together in the Broadway play Bells are Ringing at the Shubert Theater on West 44th Street from August 26 through September 7, 1957, while Judy Holliday and Sydney Chaplin were on vacation. Today, Betty Garrett lives in Studio City, California, in a home she and Larry bought in 1963.

SIDNEY SKOLSKY

ACTOR, WRITER, PRODUCER

Sidney Skolsky is best known to Jolson fans as the man who formulated the idea of making a movie about Al Jolson while a producer/screenwriter with Columbia Pictures. A native New Yorker, Skolsky became a noted newspaper columnist and press agent. His column *Times Square Tintypes,* begun in 1929, first gained fame in New York.

He moved to Hollywood in 1932, maintaining an

Skolsky with Jolson

office at the famous Schwab's Drugstore, a popular soda fountain Hollywood hangout where many talented movie beauties were first *discovered*. Among other newspapers, the New York Post and the Los Angeles Herald published his syndicated column "Hollywood is My Beat." Skolsky co-wrote the script for *The Daring Young Man* for Twentieth Century Fox in 1935. An ardent admirer of Al Jolson, he persuaded Columbia to make a movie of Jolson's life and career and approached Jolson for his blessing which Jolson gladly remitted. The film was to be named *The Jolson Story*.

Later, in 1953, Skolsky produced *The Eddie Cantor Story* for Warner Brothers.

Curiously, it was Sidney Skolsky who first placed in print the sobriquet *Oscar*, redefining the identification of the golden 13.5 inch high statuette of the Academy Awards. The story goes that the Academy librarian Margaret Herrick said in passing, that the statuette looked like her Uncle Oscar. In 1934, Skolsky referred to the statuette as *Oscar* when he wrote about Katherine Hepburn's first *Best Actress* win. In 1939, the name *Oscar* was officially adopted by the Academy.

Here are some career facts about Sidney Skolsky, to whom Al Jolson fans owe quite a debt.

1968   The Legend of Lylah Clare Actor: Himself
1961   Hollywood: The Golden Years Screenwriter
1958   Teacher's Pet Actor
1953   The Eddie Cantor Story Producer / Screenwriter
1950   Sunset Boulevard Actor: Himself
1946   The Jolson Story Producer
1941   Tom, Dick and Harry Actor: Announcer
1936   The General Died at Dawn Actor
1935   The Daring Young Man Short Story Author
1934   Hi, Nellie! Actor: Himself

JOE E. LEWIS

"You're only young once. But if you work it right, once is enough." I guess you can say that Joe E. Lewis, the famed comedian, whom some say was the funniest man who ever lived, and whose trademark song "Sam, You Made the Pants Too Long," that has been sung in night clubs from one end of the United States to the other, was a good friend to Al Jolson.

Joe E. (real name Joseph Klewan) was born on New York's lower East Side but made his fame in Chicago when just 25. In the 1940's he reached his peak as a gregarious, carefree, vagabond sort of guy, a dedicated horse player, a foe to the gangsters of that era, and a great night club entertainer. At a testimonial dinner to revise Joe E.'s failing career in

Chicago's Oriental Theater, Al Jolson sang for almost an hour, which was nothing for Al to accomplish. Song belter Sophie Tucker and cowboy stars Tom Mix and Hoot Gibson were also present to help raise the $ 14,000.00 in bonds, funds Joe E. needed at the time.

"It isn't a fortune, Joe" Jolson said apologetically at breakfast the next morning, "but it'll get you started again. You'll do all right...and don't forget, not to use these bucks for show-business. The testimonial was to stake you to a haberdashery store, wasn't it?" Al had invited Joe to come to California to stay with him. "Please, Jolie. I can't take any more charity. " "Don't mix charity with friendship. You're comin'. It's settled."

Joe E. knew Al's intentions were good, but he didn't take him seriously, regarding it as a Hollywood euphemism, like, "Let's have lunch next week."

In 1928 Jolson flew with Joe E. to Agua Caliente, along with motion picture moguls Darryl Zanuck and Jack Warner, in a chartered plane. Al even took the controls for a few minutes, being sort of an amateur pilot. The pilot left Jolie for a moment at the stick and walked back to the other guests who almost screamed. It was an unappreciated joke.

" I didn't think they would mind." Al said to Joe E.

Once, at the Cocoanut Grove night club, a drunk made an improper remark to Ruby Keeler, so Al got up and slugged him. The drunk came back at Al so Joe E., always faithful to Al, dropped him with a right cross. Everyone applauded and held up Joe E. and Al's hand declaring," The win-nahs!"

When Joe E. Lewis opened a night club called the Chateau Madrid on W.54th Street in New York without any money for backup, all his friends showed up for the opening, including the cream of vaudeville show business, Al Jolson, George Jessel, Jack Benny, Harry Richman, Jack Pearl, and Clayton, Jackson & (Jimmy) Durante. Joe E. always had lots of friends to support him.

Yes, Joe E. Lewis and Al Jolson were everyday friends. They even gambled on the fights together, always battling, always furious, always contradicting one another. Al would never agree to Joe E.'s choices, especially when Joe E. wanted to place a bet favoring Max Schmeling over Joe Louis, almost his namesake.

"You're a Yom Kippur Jew. If you bet on that Nazi bastard we're through. Through, you understand!" Jolson was mad. Hitler's purge of the Jews had begun and Schmeling was on Hitler's side. Al took Joe E.'s 500 big ones and bet it on Joe Lewis. Unfortunately, it was the first time that Louis was knocked out in 17 years. Oh, well!

"Sorry about the five hundred, " Jolie apologized. Remember, they were friends. Weren't they?

LOUIS EPSTEIN

EPPIE

Louis "Eppie" Epstein was Al Jolson's manager for nearly 40 years.

"I first met Al when he was in small time vaudeville. It was in the Academy Hotel on 14th Street. He was part of an act billed as Jolson, Palmer and Jolson. The other Jolson was Al's brother, Harry. Palmer was a comedian who had to work from a wheelchair."

Eppie was the assistant advance man for a show called *Across the Pacific.* "Money was mighty scarce. So, to help make ends meet, I got a job across the river in Hoboken, New Jersey, unloading peaches at four dollars a day, and I started work at four a.m."

One day someone told Eppie to pass some peaches off on the other side of the freight car to make extra money. He had Jolson help him and both got caught and were thrown out of the freight yard.

"Al went with Dockstader's Minstrels. He was just another end man in New Orleans, when he came to me and asked for fifty dollars so he could go back to California to see his wife, Henrietta."

Jolson went to San Francisco, a break that changed his life. "Frisco was lucky for Al. He was booked for a tour, came to the attention of J.J. Shubert and went back to the New York Winter Garden with *Show of Shows*.

"On opening night, Al flopped and was fired. But, the next day, J.C. Hoffman, director, urged that Al be given another chance. He was and the rest is history. He was a smash and practically carried the show from then on."

Eppy remained Al Jolson's manager until about 1932. Eppy was generally known as Mae West's personal manager and had even discovered the comedy team of Bud Abbott and Lou Costello while he was away from Jolson. When the show *Hold On to Your Hats* began production in 1940, Eppy returned as Al Jolson's manager and would do anything for Jolson.

Louis Epstein was a gentle man who gave his all to his client and became a link in the Jolson legend. "God made a Victor Herbert, a Caruso, a George M. Cohan, and an Al Jolson.

"Eppie" in Later Years

When Al passed on the mold was broken. In my book, he topped them all."

PART FIVE

The Songwriters and Their Songs
Finding Tin Pan Alley?

TIN PAN ALLEY

I Like New York In June,
How About You?
I Like A Gershwin Tune
How About You?

Once during an interview, composer Harold Arlen said, "A good lyric is the composer's best friend." According to Arlen, a close bond between composer and lyricist is essential to the success of any song. Normally, a song is created when the usual thirty-two bar melody is written, and lyrics (words), are added and then arranged for interpretation by a musician, a group of musicians (band or orchestra), or a vocalist, or group of vocalists. To become a song, a composition must include words. Reversing that role, a song may be defined as poetry set to music. A question may be: What came first, the chicken or the egg? The lyric or the melody? George Gershwin once glibly replied, "...the contract."

A notable composer is distinctive in melodic line and construction. A distinguished lyricist is able to formulate words for already written music which is extremely difficult to accomplish by any stretch of the imagination. Is it easier to write music to words, or words to music?

During the course of my career, I've known three songwriters. When I helped manage the NBC radio and television Ticket Division in New York back in the 1950's, I befriended a songwriter named J. Fred Coots who had written the legendary, perennial song "Santa Claus is Coming to Town" and the standards "For All We Know" and "You Go to My Head," [the latter is Glenn Millers favorite composition]. I exchanged complimentary broadcast tickets, which he distributed among his friends for personal prestige, in exchange for personally inscribed song sheets. We always wound up talking about music and how his life consisted of an unending effort to "plug" his songs in order to maintain them in performance use in order to earn royalties.

A songwriter named Joe Howard, who also wrote tunes for entertainer Beatrice Kay (mostly about the Gay Nineties), would keep me company on some days. He was down and out and aging, so what available broadcast tickets I could spare he would give to friends in an effort to restore his importance in a world that seemed to have forgotten him. Late in 1952, comedian Milton Berle, known then as Mr. Television, honored Joe Howard on his *Texaco Star Theater* television show.

During the same period I spent many a lunch hour with a young piano player who fronted an instrumental trio who performed gigs at local New York Hotels, as well as on Steve Allen's daytime, pre-*Tonight Show* television program, *Date in Manhattan*. His now familiar name is Cy Coleman. In one of the unused third floor radio studios, I would sit alongside Cy on his piano bench while he practiced his craft. I would woefully sing along. We became lunch- time buddies.

Gershwin At The Piano

I often attended those gigs at the Park Lane Hotel on weekend evenings with my friends. Cy was experimenting writing songs even then. "Witchcraft" is one of his best. Sadly, we lost Cy Coleman early in 2005.

In my first group of books, *The Best Damn Trumpet Player*, *The Song Stars*, *The Music Men*,and *Jukebox Saturday Night*, I wrote about many of the musicians, vocalists, and arrangers of the Big Band Era and beyond. None of these books could have been written unless somebody first wrote the songs these musicians played, and the vocalists sang and the arrangers orchestrated.

Some of the performing subjects of those four books also composed music or wrote lyrics at one point or another in their career: Mel Torme's "The Christmas Song", Peggy Lee "Manana," Paul Weston "I Should Care", Ella Fitzgerald "A Tisket, A Tasket," Lee Hale "The Ladies Who Sang with the Bands", Frankie Laine "We'll Be Together Again", Al Jolson "My Mammy", Bing Crosby "Where the Blue of the Night", Duke Ellington "Sophisticated Lady", Larry Elgart, the theme of *American Bandstand*, "Bandstand Boogie" and others, although they are not generally known as song writers. Some say that Jolson really didn't write anything, but lent his name to certain songs to help insure their success and to award him royalties in exchange.

Today, Tin Pan Alley is essentially The Brill Building and immediate vicinity in New York City, the singular place where music publishing offices are located and where songwriters and song pluggers congregate. The original Tin Pan Alley first centered around West 28th Street in New York City at the turn-of-the-century and up to World War I, where many of the music hall singers and vaudevillian actors once lived. There, many song publishing offices, like the old Jerome Remick Company, employed piano players to demonstrate their newly published songs for vaudeville performers who may have been searching for new musical material, and the general public at large. Early in their careers George Gershwin and Irving Berlin worked as piano players for music publishers at $25 a week.

The location of Tin Pan Alley later moved uptown to Forty-Sixth Street, between Broadway and Sixth Avenue, and when the sound of radio dominated the music business, Tin Pan Alley relocated into lush office suites beneath the shadow of NBC's Rockefeller Center, extending up to Fifty-Second Street where CBS radio was located.

The designation Tin Pan Alley, actually a sobriquet for the sheet - music publishing industry, was adopted from the tinkling, sometimes out-of-tune pianos being intensely exercised, sounding to a passerby like tin pans being drummed upon as groups of songwriters simultaneously demonstrated their craft at the offices of various publishers through sometimes open windows, and all at the same time. Tin Pan Alley was the place where sheet music was written, demonstrated, packaged, and vigorously peddled. Remember, with no radio or television, sheet music had to thrive and survive on the strength of song sheet demonstrators playing a new tune in those storefront offices of publishers who also relied upon the illustrated sheet music covers that artfully portrayed the allegory of a tune, sometimes featuring photos of a popular musician or vocalist, like the prolific Al Jolson, who had successfully performed it on stage or on recordings. To create a hit song, the axiom of the time was, "You gotta say 'I Love You' in thirty-two bars," and "keep the title short and memorable."

The participants called themselves *Alleymen*. *The Alleymen*, faced with radio companies refusal to pay songwriters for airing songs, and with restaurants blatantly playing songs without compensating their authors, organized ASCAP, the American Society of Composers, Authors and Publishers, which still solidly and securely represent the song writing community in all its aspects, monitoring use and collecting royalties for the composers and lyricists.

Of course, there are too many songwriters to portray here, and since all of the great songwriters are no longer with us, no interviews were possible.

However, one such individual is Sam Arlen, the son of the prolific Harold Arlen, whom we profiled as a vocalist in *The Music Men*. Sam keeps the Arlen lamp burning by carefully overseeing his Dad's musical legacy. Another is Jonathan Schwartz, the son of Arthur Schwartz, composer of the great standard "Dancing in the Dark." Jonathan, one of the best-known DJs in New York, is a performer in his own right, a musical event host, an author, and an acknowledged Frank Sinatra expert.

Some composers collaborated with a single lyricist, or maybe just a few, and some with many. Irving Berlin and Cole Porter were noted to write both the music and lyrics to almost all their compositions. Richard Rodgers collaborated first with Lorenz (Larry) Hart, and later with Oscar Hammerstein II. Composer Harry Warren, noted mostly for songs composed for Hollywood musicals, collaborated with lyricists Al Dubin, Mack Gordon, Ralph Blane, Arthur Freed, Ira Gershwin, Leo Robin, Billy Rose, and others. Like Warren, Harold Arlen acquired many additional lyricists when he first split with Tin Pan Alley and Broadway and migrated to California to work for the movies. After all, being work-for-hire composers, they were not always able to select their lyricists. Lyricist Ted Koehler was Harold Arlen's early, principal collaborator, especially during their two shows-a-year job at Harlem, New York's famous Cotton Club. Along the way, Arlen linked up with E.Y. "Yip" Harburg (who wrote the lyrics for Arlen's *Wizard of Oz*); Johnny Mercer, Leo Robin, Ralph Blane, Dorothy Fields, Ira Gershwin, and even author Truman Capote when he went back to Broadway for their show *House of Flowers*.

Although most of us are more familiar with the names of Irving Berlin, Richard Rodgers, Cole Porter, and George Gershwin, it must be realized that the name of Harold Arlen and some others surely belong among this unique group of musical geniuses. No one can say why the name Harold Arlen, who wrote the great standards "Come Rain or Come Shine," "Over the Rainbow," " That Old Black Magic," "Stormy Weather," and my favorite, "My Shining Hour," seems to be relatively unknown compared to the other greats. It may be argued that Arlen had perhaps too many collaborators, thus his fame was somewhat diluted. This was due partially to the lyricist selection process when he composed for Hollywood Studios, being known then as the "composer's haven."

THE SONGWRITERS

AND THEIR SONGS

JOHN PRIMERANO

Premier performer, pianist, songwriter John Primerano, hails from Philadelphia, Pennsylvania. He speaks about Jolson's songs:

"Al Jolson was, to a songwriter, the go-to-guy, that is, if you  wanted a hit song. It was known that Al Jolson's performance magnetism could create a hit with a single, live performance.

"Just ask, if it were possible, the songwriting team of DeSylva, Brown and Henderson. Ask, too, the songwriter and showman Billy Rose. And...ask George Gershwin.

"If you look closely at some of the most familiar songs associated with Jolson, you find simple, rather unsophisticated songs with a reoccurring theme...returning back home: "My Mammy," "Back in Your Own Backyard," "California, Here I Come," and "Swanee," all containing lyrics with that yearning to return home. "Rock-a-Bye Your Baby with a Dixie Melody" and "Is It True What They Say About Dixie?" may have drawn on Jolson's minstrel stage persona, yet they too convey the same longing.

John Primerano

"Should Jolson's magic with a song be written off as the product of a simpler time, perhaps a less discriminating, lower technological, or socially unconscious time? Maybe, except for one single thing: Jolson's overwhelming talent and his even stronger desire to win over an audience. Jolson's sincerity in his delivery was adored by the public, who could never get enough of him. With songs that were both hummable and sometimes heart-wrenching, Al Jolson was a *bona fide* hit maker.

"In his time Al Jolson was a songwriter's angel and America's musical voice."

In the old days Jolson had spent a lot of time in determining what goes and what does not go in a song. Many of the song pluggers on Broadway used to sneak to the downstairs room that had a piano in it at the Winter Garden and play a brand new tune for him. They waited expectantly for mighty Jolson to say whether or not the song would go, or if it was a bad song. Even if Jolson said that it might be right for another entertainer, the songwriter/plugger had some hope. But, if he said it was a bad song, they would ditch it and began work on something new.

JOLIE LOVES IRVING

With characteristic intensity in performance, it was Al Jolson who first put Irving Berlin's great song "Alexander's Ragtime Band" on the proverbial map when he sang it out on-stage in Lew Dockstader's minstrel show where it really caught on.

Earlier, in 1911, the tune had been featured in *The Merry Whirl*, a rather weak revue. The show closed leaving the song in danger of being relegated to relative obscurity, but the popularity of Al Jolson's performance quickly had it not only catching on with the public but even with other performers in shows all across the country.

Both Jewish immigrants, Al Jolson and Irving Berlin were also sons of cantors. In Berlin's early songwriting years, every songwriter wanted their song to be heard by Jolson, who, if he liked it, subsequently featured it on the Broadway stage, generating a great influence on sales of sheet music. Jolson's performance of a song just about guaranteed its success. This was the beginning of a Jolson-Berlin association and friendship that lasted their entire lives. "Writing songs to me was my business, just like any other. It's not a matter of inspiration with me at all," Berlin had said, "Generally I decide in a very prosaic way that I'm going to write something, and then I sit down and do it."

Royalties: In those days, sheet music sales were everything to the music business. There was no radio, no television, and few reliable phonographs and inaudible recordings. The publisher would sell his song to a jobber for six and a half cents a copy, then pay a one-cent commission per copy as a royalty to the composer/lyricist. Printing costs were one cent a copy; there was an advertising cost to consider; branches to maintain with staff in each; a sales force of "pluggers" or "song boosters" (sales people who sell the song to stage people and other potential users) and (payola) payments to performers to have them sing publishers songs, then an accepted practice.

Berlin deplored such methods, but was forced to pay people like Jolson, perhaps a hundred dollars a week, even though he resented it, to have them perform or plug his songs. Jolson would expect the extra fee as would any other known performer. That's the way it was in Tin Pan Alley.

"Usually," Berlin said, "writing songs is a matter of having to pay bills and sitting down to make the money to pay them with." When amateurs submitted tunes to Tin Pan Alley publishers, they were usually rejected. Some publishing houses received thousands of ideas for songs and it's a fact that almost none were used, either in lyric or melody, as it was known that even professionals found it difficult to write acceptable songs that would become popular and make a fair profit for it's publisher.

Alexander's Ragtime Band
Irving Berlin

Oh, ma honey, Oh, ma honey
Better hurry and let's meander
Ain't you goin' Ain't you goin'
To the leader man, ragged meter man
Oh, ma honey, Oh, ma honey
Let me take you to Alexander's

Grand stand, brass band
Ain't you comin' along?
Come on and hear, come on and hear
Alexander's Ragtime Band
Come on and hear, come on and hear
It's the best band in the land
They can play a bugle call
Like you never heard before
So natural that you want to go to war
That's just the best-est band what am, honeylamb
Come on along, come on along
Let me take you by the hand
Up to the man, up to the man
Who's the leader of the band
And if you care to hear the Swanee River
Played in ragtime
Come on and hear, come on and hear
Alexander's Ragtime Band

When Irving Berlin opened his show *Yip!Yip! Yaphank* at Camp Upton's little Century Theater in Yaphank, Long Island, he hired a private train and transported over fifty celebrities from New York City to attend the show, including his friend Al Jolson, comedienne Fanny Brice and humorist Will Rogers. When Berlin promoted the show in New York City, Al Jolson showed up just to help and influence theatergoers. Songwriter, producer George M. Cohan and dancer Irene Castle also attended the opening. It was a terrific success for Berlin, who worked hard to promote it.

Al Jolson also popularized Berlin's great postwar hit, "I've Got My Captain Working for Me Now," a fantasy revenge song enjoyed by soldiers returning to civilian life, later featured in the Irving Berlin vehicle film *White Christmas* with Bing Crosby/Danny Kaye/Rosemary Clooney and Vera Ellen. In 1927, involved with Berlin again, this time in the film *The Jazz Singer*, Al sang Irving's "Blue Skies," but Al's face had ghostly makeup applied and seemed to be leering beyond the camera which personified the movement of vaudeville stars to Hollywood, especially those with little film experience. Jolson was used to dynamics, motion and loudness, typical of vaudeville delivery that did not require a microphone. His antics were not suited to the motion picture screen.

But for Berlin, this was a stroke of luck, as it brought him to Hollywood where he would work writing songs for movies like most of the other former New York composers like Harry Warren, George & Ira Gershwin, and Harold Arlen. There he would reinvent his career as a Hollywood songwriter. Irving met up with an old friend, now movie mogul, Joseph Schenck, who was thriving in motion picture activities and able to help Berlin get work writing songs for the new talking/singing movies.

Berlin wrote the music for Al's film *Mammy*, a story that concerned the fortunes of a touring minstrel show, perfect for both star and composer, as it personified their personal past. This was Al's fourth film where Irving supplied the hit, "Let Me Sing and I'm Happy," which became Al Jolson's signature opening song for his many shows and radio broadcasts, and was featured in *The Jolson Story* some years later as he traveled by train across the big screen, traversing the United States, performing show after show.

What care I who makes the laws of a nation;
Let those who will take care of its rights and wrongs;
What care I who cares for the world's affairs
As long as I can sing its popular song

Let me sing a funny song
With crazy words that roll along
And if my song can start you laughing,
I'm happy...happy!
Let me sing a sad refrain
Of broken hearts who loved in vain,
And if my song can start you crying,
I'm happy.
Let me croon a low down blues
To lift you out of your seats
If my blues can reach your shoes
And start you tapping your feet,
I'm happy

Irving Berlin at the Piano - Eddie Cantor on Left Next to Florenz Ziegfeld, 1927

Berlin and Jolson, 1928

Let me sing of Dixie's charm,
Of cotton fields and Mammy's
arms
And if my song can make you
homesick
I'm happy!

Interesting note: In the song "To My Mammy" the phrases "How deep is the ocean? How high is the sky? contained in that song would later appear in Berlin's "new" hit song, "How Deep is the Ocean?"

IRVING BERLIN:

"I LOVE HIM! How can you not love someone who is as much a part of your household as a piece of bread. As much a part of your lives as sun and rain? Jolson has sung literally hundreds of my songs. He sings a song as a song should be sung... with his heart. He puts a song where a song belongs...in your heart. And so you, the people go along, sing along, with him! The interpretation of a song is, of course, important. But as the song must appeal, so must the singer."

Al Jolson would interpolate within Irving Berlin's career over and over throughout their show business lives. They became friends, played golf and went swimming together. Al attended Irving's Ambassador Hotel twenty-fifth anniversary celebration among important Hollywood moguls Sam Goldwyn, Irving Thalberg, Darryl Zanuck, among others, and was always there for him. That night someone sang Irving's very first published song "Sweet Marie from Sunny Italy."

For Irving Berlin, although he outlived his counterparts, colleagues, and even rivals Oscar Hammerstein, Cole Porter, Eddie Cantor, Fred Astaire, Harold Arlen, Jerome Kern, Victor Herbert, Ethel Merman, and Al Jolson, it was said that he became lonely and closed the world around him when all his friends were gone. His world and time had past. He hunkered down in his New York, Sutton Place apartment until he died, speaking only on the telephone. Irving Berlin once asked Fred Astaire,

Irving Berlin Played Only the Black Keys on the Piano

whom he held in very high regard as a performer and friend, " Why didn't you ever kiss your leading ladies in the movies?" Astaire replied: "Who do you think I am, Clark Gable?"

Always a showman, Irving Berlin told David Wolper, a producer for the July, 1986 Liberty Weekend celebration: "It was good. I wouldn't have changed a thing. Don't believe what you read in the press that the show was too glitzy. When I wrote 'God Bless America' they said it was too corny, but it's still around." The showman in Berlin lived on. He passed away beyond the age of one-hundred-and-one.

Here are some Berlin song titles which Al Jolson had probably sung and/or recorded at one time or another during his long career.

SONG TITLES:

"Always," "God Bless America," "Remember," "White Christmas," "A Pretty Girl is Like a Melody," "All Alone," "This is the Army," "A Russian Lullaby," "Blue Skies," "Isn't This a Lovely Day," "Cheek to Cheek," "How Deep is the Ocean," "Top Hat, White Tie, and Tails," "Say It Isn't So," "Change Partners," "I've Got My Love to Keep Me Warm," "Holiday Inn" "Be Careful, It's My Heart," "Easter Parade," "They Say It's Wonderful," and over 1000 other tunes.

RICHARD RODGERS

Al Jolson sang many a Richard Rodgers & Lorenz Hart and Richard Rodgers & Oscar Hammerstein tune in his career as the world's greatest entertainer.

Jolson and Harry Langdon in *Hallelujah, I'm a Bum*

The score of the charming movie *Hallelujah I'm a Bum* was composed by Rodgers and Hart. In this show Jolson sang "You Are too Beautiful," "Hallelujah, I'm a Bum," and "I Gotta Get Back to New York," all hits.

Richard Rodgers: "Working on the film *Hallelujah, I'm a Bum* was exciting. Jolson, who I had been told might be difficult, turned out to be a sweet man who at the time was undergoing one of his frequent estrangement's from his wife, Ruby Keeler. Later, Jolson wouldn't work because he wanted to go to the fights. I agreed to go with him if he'd promise to work with me later. So, to the fights we went (terrible ones) and then to his apartment where I rehearsed him for an hour.

"You can say he was completely cooperative, though it often took a little patience to corner him to get down to business." *Hallelujah* is considered to be one of Jolson's finest performances.

Lorenz Hart and Richard Rodgers

Hallelujah, I'm a Bum
Rodgers and Hart
The weather's getting fine,
The coffee tastes like wine
You happy hobo, sing
Hallelujah I'm a bum again
Why work away for wealth
When you can travel for your health
It's Spring, you hobo, sing
I'm a Bum
Your home is always near
The moon's your chandelier
Your ceiling is the sky
Way up high!
The road is your estate
The earth your little dinner plate
It's Spring you hobo, sing

Hallelujah I'm a bum again

Rockefeller's busy giving dough away
Chevrolet is busy making cars
Hobo's, you keep busy
When they throw away, slightly used cigars
Hobo, you have no time to shirk
You're busy keeping far away from work,
It's Spring you hobo, sing
Hallelujah I'm a bum again.

Al also recorded "Some Enchanted Evening," a Rodgers and Hammerstein tune from the 1949 Broadway hit *South Pacific*.

Jolson sang many, many more Richard Rodgers tunes over the years on his radio shows and as a guest on other programs. I'm certain much of the same material and more were performed during his endless trips singing for the troops, no matter where they were stationed all over the earth, during two wars.

IRVING CAESAR

Many believe the song "Swanee" was a great hit for both George Gershwin and Al Jolson. But, remember, it was also a hit for the man who wrote the lyrics, perhaps the most important words to

Irving Caesar

a song in both their careers. Irving Caesar's role in this appears to be understated. Absolute credit goes to George Gershwin for the music, but equal credit must be accorded one of Tin Pan Alley's best lyricists, Irving Caesar.

"Swanee" appeared on the Billboard charts for eighteen weeks and was number one for nine weeks, quite a feat in those days. Irving Caesar wrote many tunes which Jolson performed including: "Tonight's My Night with Baby," "Is It

True What They Say About Dixie?" "Elizabeth, My Queen," "Good Evening, Friends," "I'm a Fugitive from a Chain Letter Gang," "Indian River Trail," "Lenox Avenue," "Lonely Mothers On Parade," "Ma Mere," "Oh, Donna Clara," "Something Seems To Tell Me," "Swanee River Trail," "Swanee Rose," and "Yankee Doodle Blues" (also with George Gershwin). Needless to say, Jolson surely warbled many additional Irving Caesar tunes over his many years on radio shows.

GEORGE GERSHWIN

Some also say that "Swanee" was George Gershwin's most popular tune. It certainly was his first hit. And it was Al Jolson's most popular performance of a song. "Swanee" made George Gershwin famous overnight when Al Jolson sang it for the faithful at the Winter Garden.

George Gershwin and his brother Ira were brought up on Manhattan's Lower East Side. As an aspiring musician, George was told this by his friend, violinist Maxie Rosen: "You haven't got it in you to be a musician, George. Take my word for it, I know."

George Gershwin

Well, George would diligently play the piano the family had bought for Ira, who was relieved that George monopolized the used upright. As a staff pianist and song plugger in Tin Pan Alley in the house of Jerome H. Remick, Gershwin honed his piano playing skills earning $15.00 a week promoting and demonstrating sheet music.

With Irving Caesar he wrote some ditties for Broadway revues and became very respected as a pianist and composer. His first Broadway show, *La La Lucille* in 1919 was a notable revue that ran for 104 performances.

"Swanee" was a song George introduced earlier in a stage show sung by sixty chorus girls dancing to its strains with electric lights on their slippers. It made little impression on the public in that form. If it hadn't been for Al Jolson, the history of "Swanee" would have ended there. Jolson incorporated the song into the show *Sinbad* at the Winter Garden after first hearing it at a party where Gershwin was playing it. In two years it sold two million records and one million copies of sheet music earning Gershwin and Caesar royalties exceeding $10,000.00, a lot of money in the 1920s. Gershwin composed "Liza," the song Jolson's wife Ruby Keeler sang in a Ziegfeld show where Jolson rose up from the audience on opening night to sing the song as she performed it as a dance on stage. The audience just loved it.

George Gershwin is one of America's greatest composers having written such evergreens as "I'll Build a Stairway to Paradise," "Embraceable You," "Lady, Be Good," the great jazz composition "Rhapsody in Blue," "The Man I Love," "Someone to Watch Over Me," "I've Got a Crush on You," "Strike Up the Band," "I've Got Rhythm," "Bidin' My Time," "Of Thee I Sing," "S Wonderful," the entire score of *American In Paris* and *Porgy and Bess*, many with lyrics by Irving Caesar and his brother Ira Gershwin. The list goes on and on for the talented Gershwins.

DE SYLVA, BROWN, and HENDERSON

Buddy De Sylva, Lew Brown, and Ray Henderson.
From the beginning, De Sylva, Brown and Henderson had a unique working arrangement. Henderson was the composer and De Sylva and Brown the lyricists, but each provided the other two valuable, needed suggestions.

Their songs were so much a three-way collaboration that their names do not specify who wrote the music and who penned the lyrics. It was simply listed as De Sylva, Brown and Henderson on all their sheet music.

Together, these three musical geniuses wrote music and lyrics to endless Jolson hits.

BUDDY DE SYLVA

To begin, Al became interested in Buddy De Sylva and introduced some of his songs in *Sinbad*, Jolson's extravaganza at the Winter Garden Theater back in 1918. It was he who invited Al to the party where George Gershwin was playing "Swanee."

A short Jolson/De Sylva performance list is: "n' Everything," "I'll Say She Is," "By the Honeysuckle Vine," "You Ain't Heard Nothin' Yet," "Chloe," and "I Gave Her That," and additionally "April Showers," "Yoo Hoo," "My Mammy," "California Here I Come," "If You Knew Suzie," (which became an Eddie Cantor song, but was first performed by Jolson), "Keep Smiling At Trouble," and wrote the lyrics to *La La Lucille*, George Gershwin's first Broadway musical.

De Sylva again collaborated with Gershwin on "I'll Build a Stairway to Paradise," the mega-hit "Somebody Loves Me, " and "Why Do I Love You," all great songs that are still played and sung today by performers like Tony Bennett, John Primerano, and Tony Babino.

After Gershwin, De Sylva collaborated with Ray Henderson and Lew Brown. Their first joint hit was "It All Depends on You." In 1928 the team wrote the songs for Jolson's movie *The Singing Fool*, which included "Sonny Boy." Commercially speaking, "Sonny Boy" earned the greatest success of all their compositions.

The team collectively composed a long list of what are now considered standards: "Life is Just a Bowl of Cherries," "You're the Cream in My Coffee," "The Birth of the Blues," "Button Up Your Overcoat," and "My Lucky Star," all signature songs of the twenties and thirties.

Buddy DeSylva moved on to Hollywood to become an occasional producer and was involved with five Shirley Temple films and films separately with Bob Hope and Bing Crosby. As a movie mogul he produced the film *For Whom the Bell Tolls* with Gary Cooper. And in 1942, with record store owner Glenn Wallichs

Ray Henderson

and composer/lyricist Johnny Mercer, formed Capitol Records in Hollywood.

Lew Brown became a Tin Pan Alley songwriter as a very young man. Prolific composer Albert Von Tilzer wrote some music for Brown's early lyrics that permitted Brown to become established as a Broadway composer right up until the formation of DeSylva, Brown and Henderson. Otherwise, with Cecil Mack, Brown wrote "S-H-I-N-E," performed initially by Louis Armstrong, featured in the movie Cabin *In the Sky*, and was popularized by both Bing Crosby with the Mills Brothers. "S-H-I-N-E" is lastly identified with my good friend Frankie Laine, who gave it the longest run of all.

Ray Henderson, the third member of the songwriting triumvirate, became the rage of Broadway with his partners as recounted above. During World War I, Henderson found work in a band as the piano player and sold Liberty Bonds. After the war he moved from his home in Buffalo, New York, to New York City where he worked in Tin Pan Alley as a song plugger and found work as a piano accompanist for several, established vaudeville performers. He met up with Lew Brown in 1922 and the two wrote songs for the *Ziegfeld Follies* and *Greenwich Village Follies*. In 1926, Henderson composed the great standard "Bye, Bye, Blackbird," popularized by Eddie Cantor and eventually became vaudeville star Georgie Price's theme song.

Important to note: Henderson's song "Alabamy Bound" with lyrics by Ray Green, was introduced and popularized by Al Jolson at the Winter Garden. Jolson recorded it and Eddie Cantor interpolated it into the Broadway musical *Kid Boots* in 1925.

De Sylva, Brown and Henderson finally wrote their own musical *Good News*. It ran for 557 performances on Broadway and featured 16 songs from the productive team. Songs included "The Best Things In Life Are Free," "The Varsity Drag," "Goods News,"

"Just Imagine," and eleven others. The team's greatest song was, as noted earlier, "Sonny Boy." Al Jolson recorded it in1928 and again in 1946 for *The Jolson Story.*

It would seem Al Jolson owes a great deal to De Sylva, Brown and Henderson, whom, I guess owe just as much to Al Jolson.

What came first, the chicken or the egg? The words or the music? The writer or the performer?

HAROLD ARLEN AND E.Y. HARBURG

HAROLD ARLEN

Not heavily involved in Al Jolson's musical life, nevertheless, it was Harold Arlen and E.Y. "Yip" Harburg who wrote the songs for *The Singing Kid.* Besides the medley of old Jolson songs performed at the opening of the film, the original songs "I Love to Sing-A," "You're the Cure for What Ails Me," "Who's the Swingin'est Man in Town," "Save Me, Sister," and "Keep That Hi-De-Ho in Your Soul" (a vehicle for bandleader Cab Calloway) were the principle songs. Arlen and Harburg were joyfully responsible for the great songs written for *The Wizard of Oz* a few years later.

Harold Arlen eventually emerged as one of the premier songwriters ever, having composed this great list: "Let's Fall in Love," "Ac-Cent-Tchu-Ate the Positive," "My Shining Hour," "For Every Man There's a Woman," "Over the Rainbow," "That Old Black Magic," "Blues in the Night," "Get Happy," "I Love a Parade," "Stormy Weather," "It's Only a Paper Moon," "Come Rain or Come Shine," and many more, all with a variety of lyricist collaborators.

E.Y. "YIP" HARBURG

"Yip" Harburg also wrote the songs for the stage success *Finian's Rainbow.* He too, has collaborated with some of our best songwriters: Harold Arlen, Burton Lane, Jerome Kern, Arthur Schwartz, Vernon Duke and Jule Styne.

HARBURG: "Writing with different composers is always a

different psychological experience. Each one has his own approach to creation. Each composer brings out a different aspect of your work. It's knowing the person you are dealing with and the sensitivities of the two of you."

Bert Lahr, Ray Bolger, L.K. Sidney, "Yip" Harburg, Judy Garland and Harold Arlen - Rehearsing

"Yip" Harburg produced some of America's great standards: "Last Night When We Were Young," with Arlen; "Brother Can You Spare a Dime," a true Crosby classic; "How Are Things in Glocca Morra" and "Look to the Rainbow," both from *Finian's Rainbow*, among many other fine works.

Harburg returned to writing for Jolson when he composed the score to Broadway's *Hold On to Your Hats* with Burton Lane in 1940. It was to be Al Jolson's last Broadway appearance. The songs were "There's a Great Day Coming Manana," "The World is in My Arms" and "Don't Let It Get You Down." These were not memorable Jolson tunes.

Harburg, who collaborated with Arlen on the songs for The Wizard of Oz, was once admonished by an interviewer when the interviewer discovered that Harburg wrote "April in Paris" and had never been to France. "How could that be," asked the interviewer, "that you could write such a passionate song about a city like Paris without having been there to get a feel for that great city?" His reply: "Well," said Harburg sardonically, "I've never been over the rainbow, either."

GUS KAHN

The son of Gus Kahn is Donald Kahn, in his own right a songwriter ("A Kiss to Build A Dream On"), a song publisher, and a piano-playing musician, too, and the Godson and great friend of Al Jolson. His father wrote "Toot, Toot, Tootsie" for Al, (the first song performed in a talking picture), but it came the hard way, as Jolson would never let Gus Kahn in to see him, that is, until Kahn's wife to be, a song plugger who called everyday saying that Gus Kahn wanted to meet Al Jolson, and play him some songs. It was Henrietta, Jolson's first wife, who spoke to her and they became friends, leading to Jolson and Kahn eventually getting together. Kahn wrote a string of songs for Al Jolson including "Carolina In the Morning," and "You Ain't Heard Nuthin' Yet."

In his career Gus Kahn collaborated on "Liza," "My Buddy," " When My Ship Comes In," "It Had to Be You" (His best song, I think!), "Ain't We Got Fun," and for Eddie Cantor "Making Whoopee," among others, including "Flying Down to Rio," for Fred Astaire.

Gus Kahn

When Donald Kahn was a little kid, he was brought to see Jolson in *Bombo*: "And when I saw him backstage he was in blackface and I was in a panic, and he said, 'It's me, Donnie, Uncle Al, don't be frightened,' and he wiped off the blackface to calm me."

"When the song 'Liza' was written by his dad for Ziegfeld's production of *Showgirl*, a show in which Ruby Keeler starred, Eddie Jackson (of Clayton, Jackson & Durante) was slated to sing the song, but Al couldn't stand it, so he used to come into the theater everyday singing the song, and when the song was ready to place in the show, he said,' Jolie gonna sing this song,' and he did, right from the audience while Ruby was on stage doing her dance. Priceless!

HARRY WARREN & AL DUBIN

After serving in the Navy in World War I, Warren began writing songs. Earlier he had been an offstage piano player at the Vitagraph Studios.

Prolific Harry Warren wrote mostly for the movies. But, oh, what a collection of film songs from the original Glenn Miller films with Mack Gordon which included "Chattanooga Choo Choo" and "Serenade in Blue." He won an Oscar for "Lullaby of Broadway" from Ruby Keeler's starring vehicle *42nd Street* and for "You'll Never Know" from *Hello, Frisco, Hello*.

Al Dubin, Busby Berkely and Harry Warren

Harry Warren was Italian, unusual for a songwriter in those days. He also wrote "That's Amore," "I Had the Craziest Dream," and Crosby's great hit "I Found a Million Dollar Baby in a Five and Ten Cents Store."

In the Jolson mood, Harry Warren wrote the score for *Go Into Your Dance*, which starred Mrs. Jolson - Ruby Keeler. The best of the seven songs were "About a Quarter to Nine," "She's a Latin from Manhattan," and "Go Into Your Dance," with words by Al Dubin.

HARRY AKST

With the unlikely name of Harry Akst, this songwriter wrote one of the most recorded songs of all time, "Dinah" with the help of lyricists Sam Lewis and Joe Young, back in 1925. Jolsonites know

Harry better as Jolson's piano accompanist and friend who traveled with him overseas enduring the rigors of entertaining American servicemen. "Dinah" had achieved popularity when Ethel Waters recorded it and it reached # 2 on the charts. Bing also recorded it with the Mills Brothers and it reached # 1. It was also recorded by the Boswells, Fats Waller and the orchestra of Sam Donohue. Akst was an accomplished pianist and conductor. He befriended a young Irving Berlin at Camp Upton, Long Island, and collaborated with him on the song "Home Again Blues." Other notable tunes were "Baby Face" and "Am I Blue?" Al Jolson is given credit for three tunes written with Akst: "The Egg and I," "No Sad Songs for Me," and "Stella." Harry Akst wrote many tunes for movie backgrounds while in Hollywood during the 1930s.

HONORABLE MENTIONS

There were many songwriters interpolated into Al Jolson's phenomenal career. Here are some honorable mentions: Composer James Monaco wrote "Row, Row, Row" for the *Ziegfeld Follies*. Monaco blessed Al Jolson with "You Made Me Love You," performed by Al in *Honeymoon Express*. That's where Al first initiated his signature sinking to one knee and stretching out his arms. In 1916, "You're a Doggone Dangerous Girl" was a Jolson vehicle in *Robinson Caruso, Jr.* and *"Dirty Hands, Dirty Face"* was used by Jolson in *The Jazz Singer*. James Monaco became an important Bing Crosby song composer in the 1930s with "I've Got a Pocketful of Dreams," and "Only Forever," to name a few.

Tin Pan Alley alleymen Sam Lewis, Joe Young and George Meyer all wrote for *Sinbad*, that included "Rock-A-Bye Your Baby With a Dixie Melody." Con Conrad, Joe Sanders, Billy Rose, Dave Dreyer, Albert Von Tilzer, Grant Clark, Jack Yellen, Walter Donaldson, Louis Silvers, James Brockman, Jean Schwartz and Harold Atteridge also wrote excellent musical material for Al Jolson.

ROCKABYE YOUR BABY

WITH A DIXIE MELODY

SAM M. LEWIS, JOE YOUNG AND

JEAN SCHWARTZ

Rockabye your baby with a Dixie melody.
When you croon, croon a tune
From the heart of Dixie.
Just hang my cradle, Mammy mine,
Right on that Mason-Dixon line,
And swing it from Virginia
To Tennessee with all the love that's in ya'
Weep no more, my lady
Sing that song for me.
Old Black Joe, just as though
You had me on your knee.
A million baby kisses I'll deliver
The minute that you sing the Swanee River
Rockabye your rock-a-bye baby
With a Dixie melody.

It's a fact that Al Jolson sang perhaps thousands of songs over the length of his career written by too many composers and lyricists to list here. On the face of many sheet music front covers you may see the name of Al Jolson listed as composer, lyricist, or both. It is understood that Al Jolson never directly wrote a song, music or lyrics, in his life. Certainly, he encouraged, suggested, inspired, and even contributed ideas and possibly some key words, sounds, and beats to a number of these musical poets' endeavors in their quest to offer the best in music for the best performer that ever warbled a tune. With Jolson's name (and photo) on the cover of sheet music it was sure to be a guaranteed best-seller for any publisher and songwriter. We are certain Tin Pan Alley participants encouraged the practice.

SAUL CHAPLIN

The Jolson Story musical arranger and songwriter Saul Chaplin:" "Jolson had his name printed on many a song. He was one of the most notorious 'cut-ins'. A 'cut-in' is usually a top performer who'll do your song only if you cut him in on the royalties and put his name on the song as one of the writers. Since it usually guaranteed the popularity of the song, it was considered a good deal among some songwriters."

It was Chaplin who wrote the words for the final song of *The Jolson Story*. The song was not supposed to be a main song for the scene, where, celebrating his parents 50th anniversary, Al Jolson had stopped singing for a while, now started a half-singing tribute. Jolson's repertoire had nothing to fit the situation, so he suggested an old classical waltz that Chaplin also knew called "Waves of the Blue Danube." Due to time constraints, Chaplin, also a songwriter, was asked to write new lyrics for the melody, which he did in short order. Chaplin sung it *a capella* for Jolson and he liked it. The song? "The Anniversary Song," of course. Jolson then recorded a beautiful and touching version of the song for the film.

Chaplin complained that he wanted to improve his initial lyrics, since the song was to become an important addition, but Jolson, producer Sidney Buchman and everyone connected with the film loved the way Jolson first recorded it. Buchman said to Chaplin, "Don't improve it. You'll spoil it."

PART SIX

The Silents Meet the Talkies

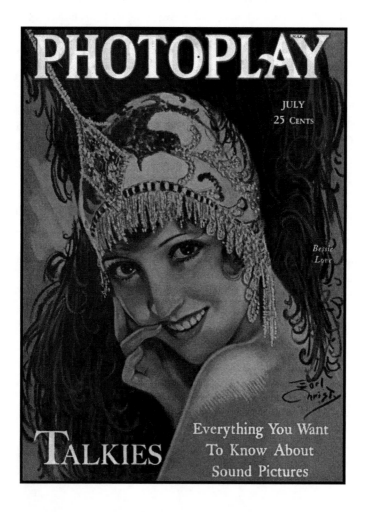

THE TALKIES

GEORGE M. COHAN, COMPOSER,

PERFORMER AND PRODUCER:

"THE SOUND PICTURES WILL NO MORE AFFECT
THE LEGITIMATE THEATER THAN THE RED SEAL
RECORDS HURT THE OPERA. WHEN CARUSO
MADE GRAND OPERA RECORDS THERE WAS A
HUE AND CRY THAT THE OPERA WOULD SUFFER.
THERE IS NO INDICATION THAT IT DID."

Al Jolson was not the first performer to appear in a movie with sound. It was in the great John Barrymore film *Don Juan*, a spectacular 1926 motion picture that first utilized sound through the revolutionary sound-on-disc Vitaphone System. Vitaphone for *Don Juan* consisted of a background score recorded by the New York Philharmonic Orchestra, and a noise soundtrack. Sound-on-disc meant synchronization was required. There were no speaking parts, but nevertheless the film sound era had finally arrived with *Don Juan*.

Sound-with-film had been around for almost as long as film itself, but due to the high costs of renovating cinemas and film stages to accommodate the installation of necessary conversion equipment, little interest prevailed so long as silent films were successful and accepted by film goers. Sound eventually came into its own due to the advent of radio, which was, of course, exclusively nothing-but-sound that became a staple in almost every home.

Earlier, Thomas Edison had developed sound with film, which was, to him, a sideline to his keen interest in sound recording. In the fall of 1894, he exhibited his Kinetophon which demonstrated film with a synchronized soundtrack that was played on discs.

HARRY JOLSON:

"Both Al and I had offers to go into moving pictures during the silent era. In 1923, D.W. Griffith made a one-picture deal with Al. When Al and I saw a few of the test shots that were made of him, he promptly canceled the whole thing and went to Europe to recover from the shock."

In 1926 and 1927 Fox Pictures, owned by William Fox before it became 20th Century Fox, tried sound in two war films, *What Price Glory* and *Seventh Heaven*. His system was later renamed Movietone. Theaters could, at that time, order film shorts, such as Movietone News, in either the Movietone or Vitaphone system. Audiences began to appreciate the primitive sound added to silent films and thus studios were encouraged to continue presenting sound-accompanied films, improving them over time.
Warner Brothers firmly decided to add sound, that included singing and minor speaking parts, to a film marked for popular musical comedy performer George Jessel, who decided he didn't want to be the first talking film guinea-pig, and, according to Photoplay Magazine at the time, also demanded too much money for the privilege. Warner had offered him $30,000, although they were under a hardship since they had already paid $50,000 for the rights to the play, so they invited his counterpart, friend and rival, Al Jolson, to star in *The Jazz Singer,* based on the original Broadway play, *The Day of Atonement*, that starred George Jessel and was currently touring during the time the film was made. Jolson, it was reported, would be partially compensated with Warner Brothers stock which he redeemed for a much greater sum when the stock rose sharply shortly after the film was released.

Unfortunately, when sound films became prolific, many popular silent movie stars were forced into retirement because their voices were either high-pitched or contained unacceptable sounding foreign accents. That included big names like Emil Jennings, Pola Negri, Ramon Novarro, Charles Farrell, and John Gilbert, all legendary silent film stars at the time of sound's conversion in film.

Luckily, actors like Ronald Coleman and Greta Garbo had

perfect screen voices that became their personal trademark and had the effect of boosting their careers. Jolson's trademark voice was already familiar to many through his Broadway and road appearances so he fared very well in the talkies.

Upon the success of Jolson's talking and singing in both *The Jazz Singer* and *The Singing Fool*, the Hollywood studios hunted Broadway for viable and useable singers, dancers, directors, choreographers, and songwriters for employment in their newly planned wave of film musicals. With large salaries and lucrative contracts they lured the best players to their studios.

The production of silent films fell silent. Al Jolson was among the first and the best of the new wave of talking picture stars.

However, later, after starring in a number of films, then becoming angry at film studios for myriad reasons, Jolson declared: "I tell you, I'm through with movies. Quitting. I'm getting out. And I know a lot of other synonyms to express the same idea, in case they don't get it. Understand, I have no quarrel with this studio or any specific studio. It's all of them put together and called Hollywood, the town where your personal popularity -- social I mean -- is based entirely upon your success at the box-office."

At the time, Jolson was lucky because he was in a unique position to quit. He certainly had enough money. And, for him, there was always acceptance on the radio, although he became unhappy with radio too, especially with sponsors telling him what to say and sing. "Well, a couple of years ago radio would be considered just as bad. But not any more."

And, there was always the stage.
Remember Broadway?: "I'd sing in a theater
50 times a night rather than make one picture."

In our lifetime, most of us have known only productions of sound films. Very few of us have lived during the era of the silents where live theater organs played appropriate and designated background music as the film flickered on the screen and titles told the story the actors couldn't.

Credit goes to the pioneers, those who experimented and explored, those who built and those who produced, and lastly, those who performed.

Al Jolson was one of those pioneers.

Anatomy Of A Movie

THE JAZZ SINGER - 1927

Warner Brothers first sound motion picture.

Starring Al Jolson as Jackie Rabinowitz (Jack Robin), May McAvoy as Mary Dale, Warner Oland as his Father, and Eugenie Besserer as his Mother, with Cantor Rosenblatt, and Bobby Gordon. directed by Alan Crosland. The story was based upon the Samson Raphaelson short story *The Day of Atonement* followed by the Broadway play *The Jazz Singer,* that starred George Jessel.

JOHN GOLDEN = *Motion Picture Magnate:*

"The Warner Brothers showed smart showmanship in putting Al Jolson in the Jazz Singer. Al had unquestionably the greatest draught in musical comedy, and he not only carried that following over to the pictures, but gained hundreds of thousands more."

ALEXANDER WOOLCOTT

New York Evening Sun:

> *"There is no other performer who holds such an absolute dictatorship over his audience. There is something magical in this power."*

The first words uttered by Al Jolson in *The Jazz Singer:* "Wait a minute, wait a minute. You ain't heard nothin' yet. Wait a minute, I tell ya...You wanna hear 'Toot,Toot,Tootsie?' All right, hold on...Lou, listen, you play 'Toot, Toot,Tootsie,' three choruses, you understand, and in the third chorus I whistle. Now give it to 'em hard and heavy. Go right ahead..."

TOOT, TOOT, TOOTSIE

Gus Kahn, Ernie Erdman & Dan Russo

Toot, toot, Tootsie, goodbye
Toot, toot, Tootsie, don't cry,
The choo choo train that takes me
Away from you,
No words
Can tell how sad it makes me
Kiss me, Tootsie, and then
Do it over again
Watch for the mail
I'll never fail
If you don't get a letter
Then you'll know I'm in jail,
Toot, toot, Tootsie, don't cry
Toot, toot, Tootsie Goodbye

You simply have to see *The Jazz Singer*. Even today, although the film is mostly silent with titles. It was the first feature film to utilize synchronous sound, named Vitaphone. It is a fine film and Jolson was absolutely grand as Jackie Rabinowitz, the Jazz Singer. Aside from pale makeup, over-expressive eyes, and primitive camera direction, Jolson comes off believable and with a great spirit. Ironically, the story mirrors Jolson's own real-life story, which is a turn-of-the century tale of a Lower East Side cantor's son who is torn between ancient tradition and modern show business celebrity. The only difference was that New York City replaced Jolson's Washington, D.C. origin.

The film demonstrates why Jolson was a great entertainer. He has the simplicity and the spontaneity of a child. He is volatile; he expresses with his whole body exactly what he thinks and feels; he exudes joy and sorrow and enthusiasm.

Yes, the film was indeed a ground breaker, but it could have been even better had they permitted the cast to speak throughout. However, the contrast between silent and talking film is punctuated here and has to be appreciated accordingly. It was inevitable that the era of silent film making was clearly over once this film hit the theaters.

One negative aspect was the constant, never-relieved distraction of very annoying and somewhat morbid, violin-strained background music, also played too fast, groaning on and on throughout every scene, inappropriately for the film's evolving story. It only paused when sound came on and Jolson performed.

The overacting techniques employed in producing silent pictures was a form of pantomime, filled with exaggerated motion and gesticulating, a substitute / replacement for the spoken word with written text on the screen. Jolson managed that extremely well and worked in his Broadway persona beautifully, considering it was his first film challenge.

> *Al Jolson*: "The first time I stood before the camera, I was so nervous that I shook from head to foot. I was afraid to move. The camera rolled, and the moment I blinked an eyelash, I thought the picture would be ruined."

SCENES FROM THE JAZZ SINGER

THE FIRST TALKING PICTURE

It was reported that the movie audience stood and cheered wildly when the film ended. With this landmark revelation in movie making, every motion picture that followed would be altered to feature synchronized sound.

Photoplay Magazine's Review of *The Jazz Singer.*
Al Jolson with Vitaphone noises. Jolson is no movie actor. Without his Broadway reputation, he wouldn't rate as a minor player. The only interest in the picture is his six songs. The story is a fairly good tear-jerker about a Jewish boy who prefers jazz to the songs of his race. In the end, he returns to the fold and sings "Kol Nidre" on the Day of Atonement. It's the best scene in the film and was a mirror of Jolson's real life.

Al Jolson In 1928:

"I don't know if Jazz Singer was a good picture. In fact, I have serious doubts. But I do know that its idea got under the skin of the audience. It even got me, when I saw the opening in New York. My wife was with me. When it came to the climax--- you remember where I come back home to sing 'Kol Nidre' for my father? ----she cried and cried. ' It's so beautiful. You couldn't be bad, and act like that. You just couldn't. Why 'I'll marry you again tomorrow!' I was too excited to answer."

Richard Watts, critic:

"Jolson and Vitaphone have triumphed over the silent drama. The important thing was that this device for synchronizing sound with cinema proved capable of catching all of that distinctive quality of voice and method, all of that unparalleled control over the emotions of an audience that is Al Jolson."

George Jessel speaks out:

"While on tour with *The Jazz Singer*, the Vitaphone was doing well, and it was agreed that I was to do *The Jazz Singer* with sound in the summer. It was brought to my attention that once the film was made, the theater version I was doing would end. I had been touring for three years. When my contract for doing the play was signed, there was no talk about a deal for sound or talking pictures. I pleaded with H.M. Warner, but he was having a tough time with financing, but was a very ambitious man branching out too far. I wanted a new deal. He talked about taking care of me if the picture was a success. I did not feel that was enough. After some heated words, he vowed I would not do the picture. Sam and Jack Warner felt we would patch up this fight, so I went to Hollywood to start work.

"My first look at the scenario threw me into a fit. They had changed the story so much that I raised Hell. Money or no money, I would not do this. That night I went down to the Biltmore theater to see my friend, Al Jolson, who was playing there in Los Angeles. I told him my story and he said I was right. However, the next morning I read in the paper that Al was going to do *The Jazz Singer*. Al and I didn't talk to each other for quite some time after that. He must not be blamed, as the Warners had definitely decided that I was out."

JOLSON'S IS NOT THE FIRST VOICE HEARD

Actually, the very first voice heard in the film was not Al Jolson's, but the voice of a youngster named Bobby Gordon who played Jolson as a thirteen-year-old.

On October 6, 1927, Warner Brothers presented the groundbreaking film at the Warners Theater in New York. In it Jolson sang "Dirty Hands, Dirty Face," "Toot, Toot, Tootsie," "Yahrzeit," "Blue Skies," "Mother of Mine, "I Still Have You," "Kol Nidre," and the closer,"My Mammy," representing the very first singing ever performed in a film.

MY MAMMY
SAM LEWIS, JOE YOUNG & WALTER DONALDSON

Everything seems lovely
When you start to roam
The birds are singing the day that you stray

But wait until you are further away
Things won't be so lovely
When you're all alone
Here's what you'll keep saying
When you're far from home
Mammy, Mammy
The sun shines East, the sun shines West
But, I've just learned where the sun shines best
Mammy, Mammy
My heart strings are tangled around Alabamy
I'se a comin', sorry that I made you wait
I'se a comin', hope and pray I'm not too late
Mammy, Mammy
I'd walk a million miles
For one of your smiles
My Mammy

The Jazz Singer was very successful to the tune of earning three-and-a-half million dollars for the Warner Brothers, great amount of money in its time. Warner's had gambled twenty percent of their assets on this film. It was so popular that many theaters held the film over the contracted showing time, subsequently forcing rival theater operators to convert to sound in order to cash in on its success and to keep competitive with other theater owners. In Europe, *The Jazz Singer* simply remained a silent film.

The Jazz Singer became an overnight sensation and was playing to capacity from Broadway to the Pacific Coast to long  lines. Over 40 million movie-goers saw the movie in one year. Jolson fans declared it was impossible to resist him doing his stuff. But, now they didn't have to go to New York or L.A. They just ambled down to their neighborhood movie theater.

THE SINGING FOOL - 1928

Another Warner Brothers-Vitaphone Presentation Starring Al Jolson as Al Stone, Betty Bronson as Grace Farrell, Davey Lee as Sonny Boy and Josephine Dunn as Molly Winton. Directed by Lloyd Bacon.

In 1928, just a year after the phenomenal success of *The Jazz Singer*, Al Jolson appeared in another part-talkie, *The Singing Fool*, in which he sings a stirring and emotional rendition of "Sonny

Boy" to a very young actor, Davey Lee, who portrayed his three-year-old son. When Jolson croons that touching song to his dying son as the child lay in his arms in a hospital, tears filled theatergoers eyes. The finale showcases Jolson in blackface emoting "Sonny Boy" again, tearing your heart out, as he absorbs his pain while performing before a theater packed with adoring patrons. This film is over 75 years old and holds up - to a point. Jolson is no actor, but, no doubt, a great entertainer.

Photoplay Magazine, October, 1929.

"Al Jolson surpasses himself. This is a better picture than The Jazz Singer, and it is guaranteed to pull your heart strings when you hear Jolson singing "Sonny Boy."

After Al Jolson sang "Sonny Boy" in that film, the song swept the country to become one of the most popular and biggest selling hits in the history of popular music. Everybody made money on that song. The story goes that Jolson had called songwriters DeSylva, Brown and Henderson by long distance to tell them he needed a heart-tugging song to sing to his child in the film. They came up with "Sonny Boy" in four hours and sang it to him over the phone. Then, there was this story told by Harry Jolson and others:

Harry Jolson speaks:

There was a feature song that Al didn't like in *The Singing Fool* so he called Buddy De Sylva, stated his woes and demanded a song.

"What is it supposed to be about?" asked De Sylva. "Well, first I am talking to a boy. Then I sing."

"How old is the boy supposed to be?"

"He is about three, and is standing at my knee."

"That's fine," DeSylva said, "I have two lines already, 'Climb upon my knee, Sonny boy; although you're only three, Sonny boy'.

Why don't you take it from there?

SONNY BOY

DESYLVA, BROWN & HENDERSON

Climb upon my knee, Sonny Boy
You are only three, Sonny Boy
You've no way of knowing
There's no way of showing
What you mean to me, Sonny Boy

Scenes From the Singing Kid
Despite Upper Backdrop

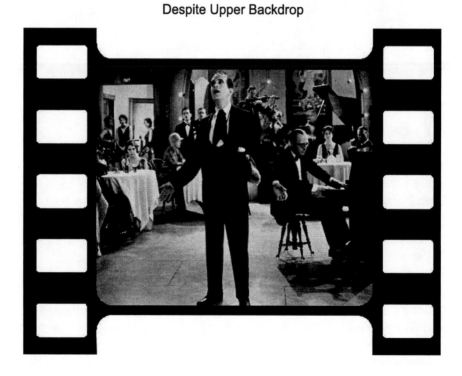

When there are gray skies
I Don't mind the gray skies
You make them blue, Sonny Boy
Friends may forsake me
Let them all forsake me
You'll pull me through, Sonny Boy
You're sent from Heaven
And I know your worth
You've made a heaven
For me, here on Earth.
When I'm old and gray, dear
Promise you won't stray, dear
I love you so, Sonny Boy!

FRED ASTAIRE, 1927, AL JOLSON WAS FIRST - WE CAME ALONG MUCH LATER:

"Walter Wanger of Paramount Pictures in New York asked Adele and I to make a screen test. We agreed, but we were not happy to do it. When we saw the results of the test and ourselves on the screen, we screamed in agony. They never offered us a contract, and we were greatly relieved."

GO INTO YOUR DANCE

With Al Jolson as entertainer-globe trotter, Al Howard and Ruby Keeler as Dorothy Wayne, all held together by a fine score from Hollywood tunesmiths Harry Warren and Al Dubin, *Go Into Your Dance* showcased Mr. & Mrs. Al Jolson starring together for the first time in this rather intricate, full-of-doubt, twist after twist, but eventually cheerful and resolved story in the 1935 Warner Brothers film. The tunes "She's a Latin from Manhattan," and "About a Quarter to Nine," were two future standards performed by the celebrity couple. With the great Al Jolson's enthusiasm and singing and Ruby Keeler's charming, but kind of awkward dancing, the film enjoyed pretty good reviews:

The film also featured popular Warner Brothers contract stars Patsy Kelly, the venerable and beautiful Glenda Farrell, famed Broadway *Showboat* singing star Helen Morgan (in a minor role plus one forgettable song), future heavy Ward Bond, famed actors

Akim Tamiroff, Phil Regan, Barton MacLane, oftentimes butler Arthur Treacher, and the films songwriters Harry Warren and Al Dubin. Later, in the early 1940s, Harry Warren would be responsible for songs in two Glenn Miller Orchestra feature films, which included the standards "Chattanooga Choo Choo" and "Serenade in Blue." "Go Into Your Dance"

would be the first and the last film that Al and Ruby would co-star in together.

The musical numbers were tuneful and well-performed, notably those built around "Go Into Your Dance," and "About a Quarter to Nine." Ruby and Al worked well together and appeared to be enjoying and supporting one another; he singing and she dancing, which fueled rumors they would be tapped for Warner's

Jolson with Patsy Kelly and the Chorus

answer to RKO's popular dance team Fred Astaire and Ginger Rogers, but that never happened. Warners allowed plenty of footage to Ruby, perhaps with an eye toward her future as a premier dancer. An Academy Award nomination for the Dance Direction of the "She's a Latin from Manhattan" sequence was garnered for dance director Bobby Connolly. The song "About a Quarter to Nine" was re-featured in the later film.

ABOUT A QUARTER TO NINE

By Harry Warren and Al Dubin

The stars are gonna twinkle and shine,
This evening, about a quarter to nine.
My lovin' arms are gonna tenderly twine
Around you, around a quarter to nine
I know I won't be late
'Cause at half-past eight
I'm gonna hurry there
I'll be waiting where the lane begins
Waiting for you on needles and pins
And then, the world is gonna be mine
This evening, about a quarter to nine

Al Jolson vigorously runs through the breezy "Casino de Paree," and "She's a Latin from Manhattan" with Ruby, as only Jolson could. The movie winds up dramatically when gangsters try to kill Al Howard and Dorothy takes a bullet for him in trying to protect him. She is to recover as Al discovers he loves her and she convinces him to finish the show. Al sings an exuberant version of "Go Into Your Dance" in blackface as the show goes on and then finishes in 1930s Hollywood style as Al kisses Ruby for the first time then reprise's "About a Quarter to Nine." Happy ending.

THE SINGING KID

With Jolson at his best, and the personal childish charm exhibited by Sybil Jason even better, *The Singing Kid* was one Jolson movie I really enjoyed. Maybe due to the film era it engaged, and it was, as Jolson would say, "corny as a deuce." I loved all the 1930s musical films, including the classic Astaire-Rogers collection.

You get to see the real Al Jolson perform here. The scenes with Warner's kid star Sybil Jason are just wonderful. I loved her work much more than that of Shirley Temple, whom I feel was overexposed and just too super-cutesy. Sybil is a natural and when she sings "You're the Cure for What Ails Me," in a charming scene, my heart was warmed, as obviously was Jolson's. Beverly Roberts was not accorded too much footage, and came in as the love interest late in the film, but I liked her too, very much. She epitomizes actresses of the era and how they were dressed and portrayed. Beverly and Sybil, still friends to this day, both live in California.

Cab Calloway did his unique musical strutting and worked within the Jolson proceedings very well. Again, Al Jolson was not a great actor, but, who can say? At least he played himself, the consummate performer, and his singing is a distinct bonus.

The songs, "I Love to Sing-A," "Save Me, Sister," and "You're the Cure for What Ails Me" are more than acceptable and even joyous and belong to the genius of both Harold Arlen and

"Yip" Harburg, also composers for a later effort, *The Wizard of Oz*. Veteran character actors Edward Everett Horton and Allen Jenkins round out the cast for this neat little Warner Brothers musical film.

YOU'RE THE CURE FOR WHAT AILS ME

HAROLD ARLEN AND "YIP" HARBURG

I was born a delicate child
Watched the other kids run wild
While they played with guns and ropes
My only toys were stethoscopes

I was a chronic " How've yuh been?"
Then like a tonic you blew in
You're the cure for what ails me
And you do me good.

Down with the "apple every day"
Down with the ultra-violet ray
You're the cure for what ails me
And you do me good.

You can go starve a fever
You can feed a cold
But I don't fear fever and I can't catch cold.
You're my pink....of con-dish'
You're my Arrowhead Springs
And my Battle Creek.Mich

I was a meekie, weakie lamb
Now I can shoulder Boulder Dam
For your smile never fails me
Hi Lady,knock on wood!
You're the cure for what ails me
What's more, you do me good.

Variety, April 8, 1936

"Spotty entertainment and one of Al Jolson's minor efforts for Warner Bros. The star should attract enough attention on his own for fair money, but The Singing Kid on its merits won't rate the customary Jolson musical grosses."

At a special 2005 tribute to Harold Arlen, who wrote this song, Sybil Jason was invited to be a special guest, but unfortunately she had just lost her beloved husband Tony and, of course, could not attend.

THE JOLSON STORY

There has been a hundred films about the Jolson era, burlesque, vaudeville, or minstrel shows, or a big night at the Palace. Some were good, but none of them could compare with *The Jolson Story*.

Producer Sidney Skolsky: "I told Jack Warner I wanted to produce a musical about Al Jolson. Warner interrupted me, 'We had Jolson when he was hot. Today, he doesn't mean a thing.' For a year-and -a-half going from studio to studio, I ran into Harry Cohn of Columbia. I told him about my dream and about Warner's response. 'Sounds interesting,' Cohn said, 'I'll get back to you.'

Four months later, the phone rang at my house. My wife told me Harry Cohn was on the phone. 'What the hell are you doing home?' Cohn asked, 'Get your ass over here. We're doing the *Jolson Story*.'

The Jolson Story, the showcase anchor of the Jolson era was my kind of entertainment. This partly fictionalized Hollywood biographical film depicting the life and times of Al Jolson is wrapped up in a pretty package featuring all the great songs and the rags-to-riches story that recalled to life, once again, the career of the Worlds Greatest Entertainer. It is musical, it is exciting, it is appealing, it's a feel

Jolson with Sidney Skolsky

good movie you will never forget.

Like many just-born Jolson fans who surfaced joyfully after viewing that film in 1947, and later fans like Tony B., who viewed it later on television's *Million Dollar Movie*, and Dolores Kontowicz, who was inspired to form a Jolson Fan Club that still exists today because of that film, and the thousands of others who discovered Jolson for the first time, *The Jolson Story* was show-business "socko", a term charmingly stated by Jolson's father in the film whenever his son's performances were declared a success.

> When the film was previewed, Jolson and Sidney Skolsky attended and the results were absolutely favorable. On the way out of the theater an elderly couple in the lobby were talking about the picture, and one said, "Isn't it too bad Jolson couldn't have lived to see it?" Jolson almost fainted.

Before the film was released, many had not figured it to be a financial winner for Columbia Pictures. Instead, it's great success lifted the studio to greater than expected success to become one of the highest grossing films of all time. Sidney Skolsky, who dreamed up the idea, had been a Broadway columnist turned movie producer. Skolsky wanted the Jolson voice, but he wanted it to come out of a young man's face. The result is as clever a synchronization job as Hollywood ever turned out.

TIME MAGAZINE
Oct 7, 1946

"The Jolson Story is a fine, noisy celebration of Hollywood's two decades of talking movies. To the embarrassment of Warner Bros., currently whopping up the 20th anniversary of sound (which they started) with some none-too-skillfull pictures, this splashy, expert piece of entertainment was made by a rival studio.

A Technicolor biography of Al Jolson, with all the nostalgic music plugged in, might easily have turned out to be an unpalatable mixture of chestnuts and corn. This movie succeeds in blending the inevitable flavors so smoothly that very young cinemagoers who *never heard Jolson - and oldsters who were never enthusiastic about him - may now understand why he was one of America's favorite entertainers during the frenzied 20s. A combination of biography and backstage musical, the picture demonstrates conclusively that box-office silk can be made out of dog-eared formulas. It is loud, costly ($2-1/2 million), overlong, occasionally trite, lushly sentimental and pretty as new brass. More important than anything else, it is uncommonly entertaining."*

Young Larry Parks, a thirty-year-old actor, pored over old Jolson records and films until he could reproduce every gesture, genuflection and grimace.

Evelyn Keyes, Parks co-star: "Larry never worked with Jolson. Larry learned to do all that Jolson singing and movement himself, working around the clock to Jolson records, and watching Jolson on film."

Betty Garrett, wife of Larry Parks: "Warner Brothers would not loan any pictures of Jolson for Larry to watch. Columbia had one picture in which Jolson had one number, Swanee. Larry had the studio set up a rehearsal hall with huge speaker and a large mirror. There he worked hours and hours with a play back man. They set up the numbers as they imagined Jolson must have done them."

Contradictory:

Larry Parks: "We (Jolson) worked hard together, and as he wanted

me to be Jolson on film as much as I wanted to be, he was invariably delighted and enthusiastic when he felt I had captured the 'Jolie' role audiences knew. Reports came that we were feuding, but they were untrue. Jolson and I were enthusiastic co-workers, with a sound regard for one another."

Musical Director Saul Chaplin Rehearses Al Jolson

NEW MUSIC! NEW MAGIC!
NEW TIMES... OF THE WORLD'S
GREATEST ENTERTAINER!

JOLSON SINGS AGAIN

A SIDNEY BUCHMAN PRODUCTION

starring **LARRY PARKS** and **BARBARA HALE**

with William **DEMAREST** · Ludwig **DONATH** · Bill **GOODWIN** · Myron **McCORMICK** · Tamara **SHAYNE**

COLOR BY **TECHNICOLOR**

Directed by **HENRY LEVIN** · Written and Produced by **SIDNEY BUCHMAN** · A COLUMBIA PICTURE

JOLSON SINGS AGAIN

Everyone who saw the great *Jolson Story* couldn't wait for its sequel, which begins where *The Jolson Story* ends with Al Jolson singing in a night club as his film wife, Julie (Ruby Keeler) walks out leaving Jolson with hope for a renewed career. It is almost three years to the day after *The Jolson Story* that the sequel was released. It was a box-office smash, earning over five million dollars. Larry Parks returns as the appealing figure who aptly represents Al Jolson and continues in his flawless effort lip-syncing Jolson so precisely. The film is a worthy match to the first.

Most of the same cast returns, with the addition of Barbara Hale, who plays Jolson's fourth wife, Erle Galbraith Jolson. They fill the screen with much emotional material which is produced and written by the same Sidney Buchman, and is directed by Henry Levin. William Demarest returns as his manager and former partner and Ludwig Donath returns as Jolson's father.

The story continues with Jolson doing a comeback and traveling abroad to entertain the troops, contracting a serious fever and meeting his fourth wife who is over 30 years younger. The songs are Jolson songs: "Babyface," "After You've Gone," "For Me and My Gal," "When the Red, Red, Robin Comes Bob, Bob, Bobbin' Along,"

"Carolina In the Morning," "Back in Your Own Backyard," among others, and even snippets of some of the classic *Jolson Story* songs.

New York Times
August 18, 1949
......The vitality of the Jolson voice is suitably matched in the physical representation provided by Larry Parks, who by now comes close to perfection in aping the vigorous expression with which Jolson tackles a song."

Variety
August 1949
"Jolson Sings Again bids fair to par. The Jolson Story grosses and may even top them. In short, a smasheroo of unqualified proportions."

Larry Parks as Al Jolson

PART SEVEN

The Theatres

You Ain't Heard Nothin' Yet

The Famous "TANK" from the finale of the Golden Garden 1910 -
New York's Greatest Spectacular - The Hippodrome

The Theaters

THE MAGNIFICENT HIPPODROME

During Jolson's time, the Hippodrome was the largest theater in America seating 6,600 people and was situated on 6th Avenue between 43rd and 44th Streets. It opened on April 12, 1905 with a lavish spectacle entitled *A Yankee Circus on Mars*. In 1906 it was taken over by the prolific theatrical Shubert Brothers but ownership was later succeeded by Charles Dillingham. Every type of entertainment was featured there. It became a vaudeville house, and in 1928 a motion picture theater known as the R.K.O Hippodrome. Showman Billy Rose opened his spectacular production *Jumbo* in 1935, but the show didn't live up to its expectations and closed in April 1936. That was the theater's last show. It was demolished in August of 1939.

JOLSON'S FIFTY-NINTH STREET THEATER

Jolson 59th Street Theater, previously named the Century

Cole Porter's Kiss Me Kate, Patricia Morrison, Alfred Drake, Lisa Kirk and Harold Lang

Theater, located on Seventh Avenue just below Central Park South, was opened by the Shuberts on October 6, 1921, as a deference to Al Jolson who appeared there in the show *Bombo*. No one up to that time had a theater named after them at the age of thirty-five. It was later renamed the Venice and housed diverse theatrical efforts from Russia's Moscow Art Theater to Cole Porter's *Kiss Me Kate* in 1948. A production of *The Student Prince* ran for 608 performances, the longest running play in the theater's history.

THE WINTER GARDEN THEATER

Over time there were Winter Garden Theaters in London on Drury Lane, and in New York, the latter originally named the Metropolitan in the 1800's. The Winter Garden of Jolson's era was opened by the Shubert Brothers on the site of the American Horse Exchange on March 20, 1911, with a musical show that starred European singing sensation Gaby Deslys. An unknown blackface minstrel named Al Jolson made his Broadway debut there in *La Belle Paree*, that starred Ms. Deslys. That was followed by his appearance in *Vera Violetta* in November of the same year and many more productions. Most of the outstanding vaudeville personalities of the era appeared there, including Ed Wynn, Eddie Cantor, and Bert Lahr. For some years afterwards, it became a

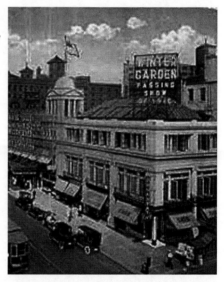

motion picture theater but returned to live performances in 1933. Musicals *Wonderful Town* in 1953 and *Peter Pan* with Mary Martin in 1954 and the immensely successful *West Side Story* in 1957 appeared at the Winter Garden, one of New York's most successful theaters. I saw *Top Banana* there in the 1950s with Phil Silvers, who sang "If you want to be the *Top Banana*, you've got to start at the bottom of the bunch." *Cats* ran 19 years at the Winter Garden Theater. It has been renamed the Cadillac Winter Garden Theater since its 2001 renovation. The show *Mama Mia* is currentlly playing there.

THE 44TH STREET THEATER

This was a theater built by the Shuberts opening in 1912 as Weber and Fields New Music Hall. It seated 1,463 people, and in its basement was housed the famous Little Club and on its roof another theater existed called the Nora Bayes, after the famous actress.

On August 24, 1925, Al Jolson appears in a revival of his Winter Garden success *Big Boy* at the 44th Street Theater, just before he began a national tour of that show, which lasted over two years, while performing in other productions inbetween at the Winter Garden.

Some of George Gershwin's first tunes were played there in

various versions of musical melodrama. The Yale Puppeteers appeared there for a while. It remained a legitimate theater and presented light opera and musical plays including a long run with the Marx Brothers in *Animal Crackers*. It was demolished in 1945 after a successful run of *Winged Victory* by Moss Hart.

The Hudson Theater

Built by Henry Harris on October 19, 1903 with the beautiful Ethel Barrymore in *Cousin Kate*, the Hudson Theater remains located at 145 West 44th Street in New York City.

The theater was furnished and considered a fine example of the new theater architecture of Beaux Arts motif. Famed producer

Kate Smith

David Belasco introduced *Nobody's Widow* in 1910, and Booth Tarkington's *Clarence* was presented and ran 300 performances with a cast that included Helen Hayes and Alfred Lunt.

In 1929, Louis Armstrong appeared in the revue *Hot Chocolates*. During the early 1950s, I remember setting up guest audience seats in the Hudson for the Wednesday night *Kate Smith Show* and other NBC television productions when I worked in the NBC Ticket Division. Earlier it was a radio studio for CBS.

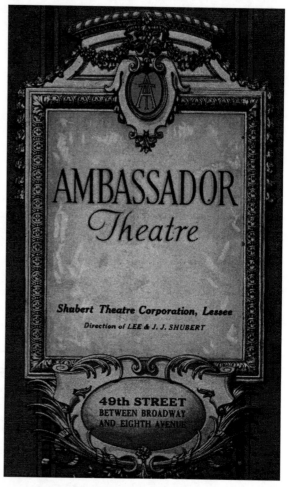

The Pulitzer Prize play *State of the Union* opened there in 1946, with Ralph Bellamy and Ruth Hussey, and in 1949, *Detective Story* was seen there. After the production *Toys in the Attic* was presented in 1960 with Jason Robards Jr. and Maureen Stapleton, and in 1963, the Actor's Studio Theater presented their initial production, a revival of *Strange Interlude* with Geraldine Page, Ben Gazzara and Jane Fonda.

The theater featured burlesque revivals until the late '60s. The Hudson was renovated in 1990 after a long, dark period, being subsumed by the Millenium Broadway Hotel.

The Hudson is one of the oldest surviving legitimate theaters on Broadway along with the New Victory, Lyceum and New Amsterdam.

The New Amsterdam Theater - West 42nd Street

You Go to the Theatre

But Have You Any Idea How Many of You There Are in New York? Do You Realize the Immensity of Theatrical Interests in New York, Compared with Other Cities?

The New York Theatre Program Corporation

Publishes The Programs of The Following Theatres

NEW YORK

Ambassador
Apollo
Astor
Belasco
Belmont
Bijou
Booth
Broadhurst
Bronx Op. H.
Casino
Central
Century
Century Roof
Comedy
Cort
Eltinge
Empire
44th Street
48th Street
Frazee
Fulton
Gaiety
Geo. M. Cohan

YOU have often heard that New York theatres are supported by visitors. That is not true. New York theatres are supported by New Yorkers. It is a fact that most visitors go to the theatre; but they constitute only about 25% of the nightly audience. Fully 75% are residents of the city and its environs.

Do you know that there are more than fifty first-class theatres in New York, whereas there are only six in Philadelphia, twelve in Chicago and nine in Boston? Few appreciate the tremendous hold the theatre has on the New York public. There is a most excellent reason for this which is discussed, in detail, in another of these informative talks.

Some idea can be gained of the number of theatregoers, through the number of theatre programs used—one copy, as you know, being given to each patron. Last season there were distributed in fifty-two theatres, over 350,000 theatre programs each week. This does not represent all the people, in New York, who go to the theatre, but the average number attending in a given week.

Globe
Henry Miller's
Hudson
Klaw
Knickerbocker
Liberty
Little
Longacre
Lyceum
Lyric
Maxine Elliott
Morosco
New Amsterdam
Nora Bayes
Park
Playhouse
Plymouth
Princess
Punch & Judy
Republic
Ritz
Sam H. Harris
Sam S. Shubert
Selwyn
39th Street
Times Square
Vanderbilt
Winter Garden
Ziegfeld Frolic

BROOKLYN
Majestic
Montauk
Teller's Shubert

The theatrical season extends, generally, from thirty-five to forty weeks, though last year there were more theatres open during the Summer than ever before. *Over 14,000,000 theatre programs were distributed in the past season.*

Of these, 25% went to visitors, leaving *more than 10,000,000* that were used by patrons living in and around New York. And remember, every one of these theatregoers paid a minimum of $1.00 for his seat.

It is from these people that practically all the stores in New York derive their patronage. Many merchants, however, do cater to visitors, but only to those who are in a position, financially, to attend the theatre.

The largest women's publication in the country has 1,700,000 subscribers to their monthly magazine. In the United States, during a period equivalent to the theatrical season, they distribute about 15,000,000 copies. So the number of theatre programs, distributed to New Yorkers alone, equals two-thirds of all the subscribers in the country, to the largest women's publication in the world.

New York Theatre Program Corporation

(Formerly FRANK V. STRAUSS & CO.)

108-114 Wooster Street, New York City

CHICAGO	BOSTON	SAN FRANCISCO
Tower Building	Little Building	Crocker Building

PART EIGHT

THE TRIBUTE ARTISTS

Clive Baldwin

Norman Brooks

Stephen Mo Hanan

Ira Green

Bobby Ermini

Rick Ryder

Rob Guest

Mike Burstyn

Richard Halpern

"Tony B."

Brian Conley

The Jolson Tribute Artists

Will the Real Al Jolson Please Stand Up

Comedian Joey Adams: "I went backstage to see Jolson at the Winter Garden. I knocked at the door and said: 'Mr. Jolson, I'm your number one fan. I sound like you when I sing. Let me go on stage with you.' My family is counting on it. Jolson said, 'Let me hear ya.' So I sang 'When the Red, Red, Robin Comes Bob, Bob, Bobbin' Along.' When I finished, Jolson asked: 'Young man, how much do you get a week?' I said $80.00 a week. He said ' I'll give you $100.00 - don't do me no more.'"

It is true that impressionists are a dime-a-dozen. There are dozens of Elvis and Sinatra impersonators abounding today. There are many Al Jolson entertainers doing the same thing. The difference is that Jolson was popular way back in the early part of the 20th century whereas Elvis and Sinatra are of more recent vintage, yet Jolson impressionists nevertheless remain in demand. All are icons of the greatest dimensions. Fans of all three are vigorously active in promoting their heroes and, for nostalgic reasons, flocking to see their heroes impressionists perform.

It has been said that anyone, as a performer, is better off as a mediocre original than as an excellent impressionist. So, since this is a Jolson book, let's look at the Jolson tribute artists and find what makes them thrive and how they managed or are managing their Jolson-style careers.

The Jolson
Tribute Artists

Who is CLIVE BALDWIN?

Clive Baldwin is a natural sounding Jolson tribute artist who sounds more like the older Jolson, even with his speaking voice and intonations. When he was only fifteen, he was told he sounded like Jolson. So he pursued the effort and performed Jolson material locally. He moved first to Canada, and then to Florida in 1968, arriving with little funds and, "Just enough money for a roast beef sandwich at Arby's."

Clive Baldwin

By 1970, he became a successful regular in Miami, Florida night clubs performing Jolson material. Clive's specialty Jolson number is "A Quarter to Nine." He learned the famous Jolson whistle from Jolson's original understudy in *Big Boy*, Buddy Walker.

"I never really had to practice my singing style, but whistling I had to practice," he said.

During the 1975 Tony Awards, he performed at the revered Winter Garden, and in the 1980s he appeared with dancers Donald O'Connor and Debbie Reynolds, both who starred in the original film *Singing in the Rain* with Gene Kelly, and together in *The Last Great Vaudeville Show*. In 1990, he performed at Harrah's in Atlantic City, New Jersey.

On Long Island, in May, 1901, Big Band Hall of Fame Bandleader Ben Grisafi recalls his fronting the band during a Clive Baldwin concert :

Ben Grisafi

"Clive was living in Florida, so we talked over the phone about his selections for the show. He sent me copies of Jolson arrangements, but some were dog-eared and faded from use, requiring my rearranging them. From the moment we rehearsed I recalled the original versions of Jolson's works in *The Jolson Story*. Clive's voice was a crisp Jolson voice. I was unable to distinguish Jolson from Baldwin. I engaged famed conductor Angelo DePippo to lead the orchestra in which I played sax along with some of the best sidemen available, veterans Frank Vaccaro on trombone and Ed Kalmy on trumpet. The show was magical."

Later, back in England, Baldwin was hailed as the World's Greatest Minstrel when he was featured in a show at the London Palladium. Baldwin not only sings and whistles like Jolson, he also shuffles that complicated little dance step Jolson performed on the runway of the Winter Garden. During the 1990s, Clive Baldwin toured Australia, Canada, England and Florida, where he settled and continued to perform.

"Having Jolson's voice has definitely helped me, but it has also typecast me, and bookers can't see beyond the voice, so it hampers bookings for my regular act."

Who is NORMAN BROOKS?

Norman Brooks did not start out to imitate the voice and bearing of Al Jolson. His natural, unstudied voice bears a remarkable resemblance to that of Al Jolson, particularly when he sings those songs that Jolson made famous. He further developed his own style on non-Jolson numbers.

Norman Brooks

"I was always trying hard not to ride

along on the resemblance," Norman stated back in 1954 for an article in the Toronto Star Weekly.

To avoid being just another Jolson impressionist, Norman refocused his career on his own material in 1953 and issued a few singles: "Hello Sunshine" and "I'd Like to Be In Your Shoes, Baby," that endeared him to his own fans and hoping the novelty of his Jolson material would wear off.

He secured a contract with 20th Century Fox and performed at New York City's Copacabana nightclub for ten weeks, followed by engagements in Boston, Chicago, and Las Vegas. At Toronto's Casino Theater and Montreal's Seville Theater, he broke attendance records. Norman appeared on TV with Milton Berle and Kate Smith in New York. Norman was but 26 at the time.

Norman had also been set as a candidate for a remake of *The Jazz Singer*, but before he could complete the test, the role was assigned to Danny Thomas.

Norman Brooks does sound much like Al Jolson, but acts more like Larry Parks, and doesn't want to become typecast and thereby lose other unrelated roles. The question at the time was: It was a toss-up whether he is better as Brooks or Jolson. In both voices he was good, but wisely chose the tougher job - to sell himself as Norman Brooks before swinging into Jolson.

In the 1956 film *The Best Things in Life Are Free*, Norman crooned "Sonny Boy" as Al Jolson, and in the 1965 film Ocean's Eleven, Norman sang "I'm Gonna Live 'Til I die." He was also heard in the Woody Allen film Zelig, singing "I'm Sittin' On Top of the World."

WHO IS STEPHEN MO HANAN?

As Jolson Webmaster Marc Leavey said, "He's not Al, Norman, or Ira. He's Stephen...Stephen Mo Hanan, to be precise. But, for two hours his is the image and spirit of The World's Greatest Entertainer."

This Jolson show was a restructured version of the

renowned *Barry Gray Show*, the show where Jolson appeared live on radio WOR in New York at four o'clock one morning in October, 1946, right after *The Jolson Story* began its run at the Radio City Music Hall when he sang to Harry Akst's piano to a small, live audience while being eagerly interviewed by an awed Barry Gray. Mo Hanan's voice may not be perfect Jolson, but he played Al Jolson perfectly, capturing Jolson's stage presence, dancing, singing, eyes rolling up, hands projected, all up a runway, emulating Jolson's glory days at the famed Winter Garden in a show he called *Jolson & Co.*

WHO IS IRA GREEN?

Another Jolson tribute artist was the late Ira Green, of St. Petersburg, Florida. He was known as the The Living Legend of Al Jolson and has performed prolifically. "I don't claim to be the worlds greatest imitator of Al Jolson. What I do is strictly my interpretation of the total man and performer as I perceive him. It doesn't come naturally to me and it takes a lot of hard work. But, when I get that applause or standing ovation, it's worth every minute of it." Ira was always a Jolson tribute artist from his earliest days singing for relatives and throughout high school. A real estate businessman by trade, Ira Green performed at clubs and restaurants throughout the seventies. He has performed at Jolson society shows and conventions over the years and has received well deserved applause and support.

WHO IS BOBBY ERMINI?

In 1993 Bobby Ermini performed great Jolson tributes at the Red Blazer Too, on West 46th Street in New York. Bobby has played alongside comedian Joey Adams, bandleader and great performer Cab Calloway, famed singer Arthur Prysock, and our own Joe Franklin. His resonant singing voice made him one of the best

Al Jolson sound-alikes.

WHO IS RICK RYDER?

Rick Ryder played Al Jolson in 1999 in the show *The Jazz Singer* at the Jewish Repertory Theater at Playhouse 91. The production paid warm homage to past productions, including the original movie. Ric's voice did not compete with Jolson's or other impressionists we know, but his acting made up for it.

WHO IS ROB GUEST?

Rob Guest performed in a terrific Jolson show in Sydney, Australia at Her Majesty's Theater in 2000. He sang twenty Jolson tunes with Jolson's gravely-like voice behind a fifteen piece orchestra and received favorable reviews.

WHO IS MIKE BURSTYN?

The son of two Yiddish theater stars, Lillian Lux and Pesach'ke Burstein, Mike Burstyn began his stage career at the age of seven in Argentina. Mike recently performed in the National road company of the musical *Jolson*. Mike has done Broadway well having starred as Tevye in *Fiddler on the Roof*, as Nathan Detroit in *Guys and Dolls*, and the documentary about Mike's family *The Komediant*, won the 1999 Israeli Oscar.

He is also a popular television actor having appeared in *Law & Order*, *Dog Watch*, *The Cosby Mysteries* and *As the World Turns*, and back in 1978 had his own TV show in Holland.

Mike's rendition of Jolson is unique as he had the same space between two front teeth as Jolson had.

Who is RICHARD HALPERN?

I witnessed a terrific performance by Richard Halpern at the Oceanside, New York Jolson get-together in August, 2005. Richard  sang and danced as show business legend Eddie Cantor in the company of one of Eddie's daughters, Janet Cantor Gari, and grandson Brian Gari as they watched and enjoyed Richard's nostalgic presentation. He was captivating performing Cantor's signature vaudeville walk-dance and hand gestures while singing some of Cantor's famous songs, including "Making Whoopee." However, Richard, known as Mr.Tin Pan Alley is also a polished Jolson impressionist, and a first class Mike Meyers' *Austin Powers* impressionist, as well.

Richard carries his audience back to the era of Tin Pan Alley, a time from the turn of the century through the 1930s. He has carried his craft through countless appearances in places like The Queen Mary, the famed Orpheum Theater in Los Angeles, and music festivals all over the country, including the ultimate venue, Lincoln Center in New York.

The Los Angeles Classic Jazz Festival reports he is the Master of Tin Pan Alley, thrilling audiences as he sings and dances with the snap and pizzaz that would make Jolie proud.

Halpern revives the timeless classics, songs that have been long neglected by today's artists and clearly overshadowed by rock and other tasteless material in vogue today. Like Jolson and Cantor and others of that genre, Richard Halpern is one of their voices from the past who delights the crowds gathered to see him perform. His vitality and showmanship are a nostalgic mirror of the days of Eddie Cantor, George M. Cohan, Fanny Brice, Sophie Tucker, Milton Berle, and the greatest of them all, Al Jolson.

Eddie Cantor or Richard Halpern. Guess who?

The Tony B. Effect

Pearl Sieben in The Immortal Jolson..."First God made Jolson, then he made Judy, and then he broke the mold."

Then Tony B. came along.

Norman Brooks, famed Jolson impressionist, celebrated his 77th birthday on August 19, 2005. One of England's prolific stars of radio, television and motion pictures, Norman is most famous over the years for his quality Al Jolson performances.

Clive Baldwin followed as a Jolson impersonator and has appeared all over the country singing Jolson material, attracting crowds everywhere.

Today, Tony B. continues in the same tradition, having emulated in song the exact sounds and voice of Al Jolson, ever since he was a kid of fifteen right up until today at the age of 45.

During lunch at an Al Jolson get-together in Oceanside, Long Island, in late August of 2005, I sat alongside Tony Babino's mom, Maria, and his Aunt Carol, both of whom were instrumental in formulating the career of Tony B., as he is known to the world of

The Trumbull Times, Conn.

"When Tony Babino started to croon as Al Jolson, the packed house stopped breathing. You could have heard a pin drop...and when he dropped to his knees, all you could hear was a fabulous rendition of 'Sonny Boy.'"

show business. While Tony sang his Jolson heart out for an hour and a half, his mom whispered the words in sync as if to guide him from the wings, much like theater prompters would do in legitimate theater productions. Of course, she was simply endearing herself to her son's efforts in a very proud manner.

After lunch and some introspective interview conversation during a 2003 interview at the famed Three Village Inn in Stonybrook, New York, Tony provided my wife Madeline and I with an impromptu *a capella* version of Jolson singing "When the Red, Red, Robin Comes

Tony B. with Richard Grudens, 2005

Bob Bob Bobbin' Along." Well, the power and phrasing, as well as the distinctly accurate performance was truly amazing. As we applauded, we became aware of a sizable gathering that had worked their way into our dining area, when they heard Tony's powerful interpretation of the great Jolson resonate without a microphone throughout this colorful, old inn.

In May of 2005, Tony joined with Italian crooners John Primerano, Filippo Voltaggio, Remo Capra, and Roberto Tirado to perform on *Italian Crooners Day*, designated by Jerry Vale and held in Stonybrook, New York, all in honor of my book *The Italian Crooners Bedside Companion* in association with WALK AM Radio, also celebrating Luisa Potenza's *Italia Mia Hour*. Besides crooning his best Italian evergreens for the enthusiastic crowd, Tony B. performed a terrific, unscheduled Jolson number, a rousing version of "California Here I Come," unsettling the mostly mature Italian audience who began gasping with disbelief, then reacting with thunderous applause, something Tony has continuously earned since 1985 when he professionalized his Jolson act. Now they knew how it was when Jolson performed at the Winter Garden and crowds cheered his act and his songs. It was almost like being there! Tony B. truly dazzles them as Al once did.

> *Tony B. might just be the classic trailblazing, high-energy vocalist of the new Millennium. His qualifications match those of all the up-and-coming singers of past generations, in a time identified as before and during the Big Band Era, and beyond. Those were the days when the great Al Jolson and the prolific crooner Bing Crosby had established the era of the vocalists and cleared the way for followers Frank Sinatra, Perry Como, Jerry Vale, Don Cornell, Eddie Fisher, Johnny Mathis, Vic Damone, Al Martino, Tony Bennett, and a dozen worthy others.*

In his quest for excellence in performing Tony B. has carefully surrounded himself with qualified people in his arena, from personal manager Robert Rosenblatt, who has provided unwavering support in matters both legal and career; to arranger and premier piano accompanist Richie Iacona, whose arrangements, as Tony B. says: " ...breathe new life into classic standards, but give my own original compositions the edge they need to stand on their own within the genre."

His friendship with the incomparable Connie Haines, who sang shoulder- to -shoulder with Frank Sinatra in the bands of Harry James and Tommy Dorsey for three years as they grew together in performing all those great songs, has bolstered Tony B.'s career to an even higher plateau. He sang with Connie in Florida before over ten thousand fans:

Tony with Connie Haines 2003, *Photo Ben Grisafi*

"From the moment I met Connie, she took me under her wing and made me feel like family. She is a wonderful and beautiful person, and her talent is second to none. That lady can swing, baby! When we'd perform in Atlantic City night after night she'd invite me up on stage, not only to perform, but to share the spotlight. There aren't too many performers in this business who would extend an opportunity like that to someone new. May God bless, and keep Connie Haines, always."

Tony B. began singing at a very young age after first being impressed by Bobby Darin's knockout recording of "Mack the Knife" and, later, after hearing the entire score of *The Jolson Story.* He also worshipped heroes Frank Sinatra, Tony Bennett, and Paul McCartney. Tony's power and production are overpowering and contain a punch that knocks you out.

Maria Babino:

"When Anthony was growing up it was during hard times for a kid, you know, with the long hair and the disrespect of elders, so I told him 'if you grow long hair, I'll cut it off when you are sleeping.' But Anthony said, 'Don't worry mom, I don't like long hair.' He stayed at home and wrote his songs, songs that his own children play for him today. "I always say, thank you God, for the blessings Anthony has brought to me over the years, as a kid, and now as an adult. I get a great feeling when I hear him sing - I have to hold back my tears. "Once, when he had an offer to go with a promoter, I prayed that he would decide not to go, because I wanted him to make his own decision about his life. And, thank God, he decided not to go. I had a bad feeling about the deal he was offered. My prayers were answered."

During his youth, both his grandfathers guided him, nurtured him and protected him, giving him confidence and poise. "They had a place in Rocky Point, Long Island, where Anthony would spend summers with them. Another blessing, Richard. Another blessing!"

Tony: "I became interested in Al Jolson when I was just a kid. I was watching the *Million Dollar Movie* on our local Channel 9. They used to run the movie for an entire week, once during the day and once at night. One day *The Jolson Story* came on, and from that moment, even though I was just a kid, I wanted to locate all the Jolson music that I could to listen to. I thought he was phenomenal. I think I watched every show that week. I was transfixed on Jolson and his music for life."

Daily Variety, Los Angeles, Cal.

"Babino worked the crowd with yet more Jolson favorites and drew such a response that Irving Caesar, who wrote the words to 'Swanee,' stood up from the dais and yelled 'You're great.'"

The phenomenon of the Beatles eclipsed his fixation on Jolson for a while. Some years later, at his Aunt Carol's home, Tony discovered a Jolson album and played it and began imitating him until he had memorized every nuance of every song.

"I bought some more Jolson material and began memorizing just about every song he ever recorded. I became obsessed with Jolson. I could even whistle like he did. I was in love with his songs and the way he sang them. After a while, people began to say that I sounded like Jolson. That's how it all started. Today, I continue to sing Jolson at almost every performance."

Up to now, Tony B. has performed at just about every important venue in Atlantic City. His mounting credits to date, span numerous personal performances, recordings, and total involvement in his trade. His recording of the Harold Arlen standard "I've Got the World on a String" was selected by Arlen's son, Sam, and his wife Joan, to be included on a Harold Arlen Songbook album, sharing tracks with Tony Bennett, Faith Hill, Eric Clapton, Jane Monheit and Natalie Cole. He is featured on the opening track. And, with a new twist singing for the movies, Tony's rendition of "The Little Drummer Boy"

Tony B. at the "Italia Mia" Luncheon, 2004 - *M. Grudens Photo*

heard at the opening of the film *The Ice Harvest* is indication enough of what Tony's future will be like.

Tony B. credits his wife for the full time expansion of his career as it stands today:

"Elayne encouraged me to go full-time after I experienced a negative, life threatening event in my life. She is the reason I have decided to expand my career and try to make it in this business. So far, so good. And I keep working at it day by day, week by week. Elayne is one hundred percent behind me. And for that I am grateful."

Tony and Elayne's two boys are already steeped in music. Anthony, 18, has been playing guitar since he was 9 years old, and Steven regularly appears in stage shows whenever he can, recently performing in a company of Frank Loesser's *Guys and Dolls* . Tony B. is setting a standard for his kids as Al Jolson, and later Frank Sinatra, set the standard for him. So, the music goes on, Jolson and otherwise.

Brian Conley
England's Jolson

**JOLSON - THE MUSICAL
STARRING BRIAN CONLEY
FROM AN ORIGINAL IDEA BY MICHAEL FREEDLAND
DIRECTED BY ROB BETTINSON - 1995**

In his early years Brian Paul Conley lived in Kilburn, although he was born in Paddington Hospital, West London. Like Al Jolson, Brian always wanted to be an entertainer. Since then he has done it all, including a tour with Bob Hope finishing with a performance at Royal Albert Hall,

and has entertained at Prince Charles Fiftieth Birthday Bash; starred in *Me and My Girl*, and performed in *Jolson, the Musical* for a year in London and in Canada for six months. He has also played in a string of light television shows for which he won awards. He played the live pantomime figure "Buttons" in *Cinderella* for three years, and in 1999 hosted the BBC Lottery Show *We've Got Your Number*. He is a fine actor, singer and pantomime artist and appeared on his own *The Brian Conley Show*, and finally saw the release of his first feature film *Circus*.

Brian Conley is one of Britain's best-loved entertainers

whose talents have earned him the prestigious Variety Club Award. *Jolson, the Musical* was produced in London at the Victoria Palace in 1995.

"I had played a year earlier in the hit musical *Me and My Girl* and I wanted to be back in a new show as quickly as possible. Many ideas were explored, considered and rejected until the idea of Jolson, and creating the part of the Greatest Entertainer the world has ever seen came into our thinking."

To begin with, Brian wasn't sure he could re-create the legendary Jolson: "Could I sound like him? Could I do the accent? Could I do justice to this great man?" Performing eight shows a week, which this role required, was an enormous challenge. It needed a performer with considerable stamina and energy.

"I had to do it! My first professional job was singing a Jolson medley in a Kilburn pub for five pounds. So you see what I mean." In England, long time International Jolson Appreciation Society member, Stan Ball, furnished Brian with films, cassettes of Jolson talking and singing, documentaries, books and other assistance, so he could learn to closely imitate Jolson's voice and emulate his performance moves. Then Brian flew to New York to visit the Shubert Theater Museum where he could personally view original photographs of Jolson, including letters, contracts and other memorabilia.

"It was amazing to hold papers with his actual signature on them and then to walk through Times Square to the Winter Garden where he held court and entertained his followers." After almost two years of planning, rehearsing, singing, acting and dancing up to twelve hours a day, they were ready. Then finally, the opening and the resultant standing ovations.

"I am privileged to be working with a talented crew and cast, whose efforts made this a great show."

Jolson was Brian Conley's biggest challenge. "I wanted to capture some of the magic of this great man, Al Jolson. I was gratified that the audience believed that it was really Al Jolson up on stage."

Stan Ball
Meets Brian Conley

by Stan Ball

Reading "The Sun" newspaper at my home in Aylesbury,

Buckinghamshire, England, I noticed an article by columnist, Gary Bushell stating that English entertainer, Brian Conley had been offered the part of Al Jolson in an upcoming stage musical to be called *Jolson*.

It planned to open in the English provinces, firstly in Plymouth in the West Country, then move to Birmingham in the Midlands and, if successful, to London's West End. I was intrigued to read a quote from Conley saying he was excited about playing Jolson, especially since he'd learnt that "Al Jolson had EIGHT wives."

As an ardent fan of Jolson's since the age of eleven, and who had painstakingly researched his life story, this came as a shock, as Jolie had four wives. Knowing Brian Conley as a comedian on our television screen, I decided to write him a humorous letter stating that even KING HENRY THE EIGHTH had not been that greedy with matrimony.

I could not envisage Conley portraying Jolson faithfully and felt he

Val and Stan Ball with Brian Conley

might turn Al's life story into some exaggerated comedy show. In my letter I teased Brian saying if he did play the role he would probably be disappointed to find he only had four glamorous leading ladies to seduce into marriage within the show.

My letter was mailed to Brian's agent, and I didn't really expect a response. Long after I had forgotten about the matter, I received a phone call from someone who identified himself as "Al Jolson", which came as quite a shock, since Al had passed away in 1950. Naturally, I questioned the caller's identity further, but he kept insisting he was "Al Jolson" and when he sensed my patience was running out, he finally confessed that he was Brian Conley.

Dumbstruck, that such a famous personality should be phoning me, I didn't really believe it was him and felt I was the subject of some protracted joke possibly from my friends in The International Al Jolson Society. My caller said he was well compensated as a comedian but since receiving my letter about Jolson, his wives, and the fact that he would be deprived of some partners he would have in his stage concubine, he hadn't stopped laughing. He said that he felt I could be a great help to him in studying for his role. At this point I realized my caller was really Brian Conley. We discussed how he would portray Jolie. He was

adamant that he would do him justice, including the use of black face make up, despite expecting some opposition to this in these "politically correct" times. Brian admitted that he knew little about "the worlds' greatest entertainer" and asked me to help him study for his role. He asked for items that would help including books,  films, records and tapes related to Jolson, and I realized just how seriously he was taking his part and how deeply he intended to research the life and music of the man he was destined to portray.

Brian was very happy to receive all the Jolson items I sent to him, but was especially concerned about his singing voice. He had heard of an American entertainer who he knew I had worked with and who had, through some quirk of nature, possessed a singing and speaking voice almost identical to Jolson. I reassured Brian that the part required someone who was basically a good actor, who had a passable Jolson-like singing voice, rather than someone with the true Jolson voice who couldn't portray the man himself. Also, I pointed out that Brian was well-known to British audiences through his television shows and could easily fill the theaters, whereas the American was virtually unknown in Britain.

Brian, used to dealing with show business moguls and their "Ten percent" offered me a monetary incentive and was puzzled when I refused. I declared that my reward would be the show's success and in seeing the name of Jolson up in lights on a prominent London Theater.

Brian worked extremely hard preparing for his role, and through this relationship my wife Val and I became friends with Brian, his Mum, Pauline and his Dad, Colin.

Val and I were unable to attend the opening show at the Victoria Palace Theater in London's West End. This night was graced by stars, including Evelyn Keyes, who portrayed Mrs. Jolson in the film *The Jolson Story* The show received great reviews and Brian grew in confidence in the role and the show became a fantastic success. Later, I got my wish to attend a performance with my wife,

Brian Conley, Erle Jolson Krasna, John Alexander and Stan Ball

and felt proud seeing the name Jolson up in lights.

Brian's Jolson voice was more than competent for the role, though there was some criticism from a few Jolson purists. From the start of the show's run Brian captivated the audiences, having them almost eating out of his outstretched Jolson hands, especially when he belted out the famous song "Mammy" to an enthralled crowd. I was immensely proud too, and for my help he gave me printed credits in the show's program. Following the show's phenomenal success in London, it went on the road and toured New York, Toronto, Canada, and with a replacement in the lead role, in Australia.

This unique experience enabled me to use my Jolson knowledge and memorabilia collection to great benefit and bring the name of Al Jolson back once again to the forefront of entertainment. It was pleasing to see his name in lights once more, nearly fifty years after he died, when the lights of Broadway were turned off in his honor. For his admirable performance, I recommended that Brian should receive an award, similar to my own, as an Honorary Member of the Jolson Society. This was approved unanimously, and I was to present him with this high honor, which would be covered by television and showbiz media magazines.The award show's producer asked for my advice about enhancing the presentation and I jokingly suggested they contact Jolson's widow, Erle Jolson Krasna, in Switzerland and ask her to join me for the ceremony. Erle knew of my work for the Jolson Society as we had exchanged correspondence, but I doubted my suggestion would be taken seriously.

"Tell her Stan Ball would love her to come over, see the show and help me present Brian's award", I urged the producer. My invitation was conveyed to Erle, she accepted, and we got together for the first time at the theater. Recently she had a cataract operation, but it was still possible to see those twinkling eyes and the beauty of the lady who stole Jolie's heart many years before. This meeting with Erle joyfully wrapped up my ongoing experiences in the IAJS.

In 1996, *Jolson*, starring Brian Conley, received one of the most prestigious honors in British showbiz, *The Laurence Olivier American Express Award*.

These days, Brian Conley prefers to enjoy family life with his wife Anne-Marie and their two lovely daughters. However he recently had a very successful run in *Chitty, Chitty, Bang, Bang* at the London Palladium.

The Victoria Palace Theater

In 1910, Frank Matcham's Victoria Palace was built at the huge sum of £12,000. However, there has always been a theater on the same site since 1832. The theater hasn't changed much since 1910, retaining the magnificent sliding roof, a simple and still effective precursor of air-conditioning. Today, the gray marble foyer with its old gold mosaic and pillars of white sicilian marble is again much as it was in 1910.

My Brian Conley/Jolson Story

By Max Wirz

I was born in 1934 and raised in Kreuzlingen, near the Swiss/German border. As I heard my elder siblings tell in later years, my first encounter with Al Jolson must have been subconscious, heard in my mother's arms, while she swayed me back and forth, calling me "My Sonny Boy." My mother must have picked up that name while listening to American-based radio broadcasts.

When World War II ended, I was eleven. There were three movie theaters in our town then, the Bodan, the Apollo, and Central, showing a weekly double-feature of cowboy and gangster B-movies.

Practically all of these films were American, with few in English and French. All were run in their original languages with sub-titles in German and French. There was one obstacle though; you had to be "confirmed" as 16 years old to be allowed to go to the movies. This was a silly rule, because those cowboy, gangster and Tarzan movies, even Abbott and Costello, Laurel and Hardy, and the Three Stooges, which we were not permitted to see, I saw on day-time American television during the fifties.

One Sunday afternoon, while watching Johnny Weissmuller in *Tarzan and the Leopard Woman*, I, and two dozen more 14-year-old students were caught and punished. On a free Wednesday afternoon we had to report to school and write an essay "Why do I go to the movies."

With the help of my oder brother Hans, who let me borrow his long pants, I was nevertheless able to sneak into the Central or Bodan on Sunday afternoons. For me, this was an excellent opportunity to hear American English spoken. At about that time, (1947-1948) I discovered the American Forces Network radio stations in Frankfurt, Suttgart and Munich, which introduced me to the music of the 30's and 40's and which helped me in my efforts with English. Although I did not understand all that was said, shows like "*Fibber McGee and Molly* and *Amos and Andy*, and *Arthur Godfrey's Talent Scouts*,

Swiss Radio Personality Max Wirz

and news compiled by AP, UP and INS, gave me a feeling for the language.

In 1950, *The Jolson Story* with Larry Parks was featured at the Bodan theater, and now it was legitimate for me to attend. I was pretty good in English and could understand much of it without keeping an eye on titles. I went to see *The Jolson Story* four times and could memorize the songs, especially "April Showers." Ever since 1986, when I started producing and presenting radio programs as a freelance disk jockey, "April Showers" has become a standard in my first show during the months of April, and will be so for as long as I am on the air.

I know I am in good company as an admirer of Al Jolson

ever since Frankie Laine told me in an interview at his home in San Diego, that as a schoolboy he skipped school one afternoon to see *The Jazz Singer* and listen to LPs and CDs we've picked up over the years, including a walk-on performance on a Bing Crosby radio show.

A few years ago, while visiting London, we took in the musical *Jolson* with English actor/singer Brian Conley. The story followed pretty much *The Jolson Story*. We thought that Brian Conley's performance was excellent. The brashness of his appearance, as he entered the theater from the rear, the voice and mannerisms resembled those we have seen in movies and clips of live TV performances of the one and only Al Jolson. Now I understood why this man Jolson was such a long time favorite and earned the title of The World's Greatest Entertainer.

I will continue to present Al Jolson's exceptional songs to the audiences of RADIO EVIVA in Switzerland and HAMBURGER LOKALRADIO in Hamburg, Germany.

They "ain't heard nothin' yet!"

Special thanks to *The International Al Jolson Society* for their invaluable assistance and cooperation in the formation of this book.

**Jan Hernstat
PRESIDENT**

Dolores Kontowicz
(Founder) - 1950-1958
and 1991-1995

The International
Al Jolson Society

246 Chance Drive
Oceanside, NY 11572

To Join:
www.jolson.org
Dr. Marc Leavey, Webmaster

INTERNATIONAL · AL JOLSON SOCIETY ·

Harry Rhinehart
1983-1987

Irvin Warwick
1958-1979

Past Presidents

Mike Modero
1987-1991

Stan Gerloff
1979-1983

John Wehrman
1999-2003

Bruce Wexler
1995-1999

Jolson Bibliography

Adams, Joey, *Here's to the Friars*. New York, New York: Crown Publishers. 1976

Allen, Fred, *Much Ado About Me*. Boston, Mass: Little, Brown and Company. 1956

American Magazine, Al Jolson Interview. "If I Don't Get Laughs and Don't Get Applause, {The Mirror will show me who is to blame.} New York, New York: April 1919

Anderton, Barrie, *The World of Al Jolson*. London, England: Jupitor Books. 1975

Barrymore, Lionel, with Cameron Shipp. *We Barrymores*. New York, New York: Appleton-Century Crofts. 1951

Benny, Mary Livingstone, with Marcia Borie and Hilliard Marks. *Jack Benny-A Biography*. Garden City, New York: Doubleday & Company. 1978

Bergreen, Laurence. *As Thousands Cheer*. New York, New York: Penquin Books. 1991

Briggeman, Jane. *Burlesque. Legendary Stars of the Stage*. Portland, Oregon: Collectors Press Inc., 2004

Cohn, Art. *The Joker is Wild*. The Story of Joe E. Lewis. New York, New York: Random House. 1955.

Crosby, Bing with Pete Martin. *Call Me Lucky*. New York, New York: Simon & Schuster 1953

Evans, Philip R., and Kiner, Larry F., *Al Jolson-A Bio-Discography*. Metuchen, New Jersey: Scarecrow Press, Inc. 1992

Ewen, David. *American Songwriters*. New York, New York: H.W. Wilson Company. 1987

Fisher, James, *Al Jolson - A Bio-Bibliography*. Westport, Connecticut: Greenwood Press. 1994

Goldman, Herbert G., *Jolson-The Legend Comes to Life*. New York, New York: Oxford University Press. 1988

Griffith, Richard. *The Talkies*. Articles From Photoplay Magazine. New York, New York: Dover Publications.1971

Gerloff, Stan. Editor, *The Jolson Journal*-all Issues. Oceanside, New York: International Al Jolson Society. 1950 To present. 2005

Giddens, Gary. *A Pocketful of Dreams*, The Early Years. New York, New York: Little Brown & Co. 2001

Grudens, Richard. *Bing Crosby-Crooner of the Century*. Stonybrook, New York: Celebrity Profiles Publishing. 2003

Grudens, Richard. *The Music Men*. Stonybrook, New York: Celebrity Profiles Publishing 1998.

Hanks, Stephen. *Jolie's Greatest Radio Show*. New York: Fall, IAJS Journal. 1996.

Jason, Sybil, *My Fifteen Minutes*, Boalsburg, Pennslyvania: BearManor Media. 2005

Jessel, George. *So Help Me*. Cleveland, Ohio: World Publishing Company. 1944.

Jessel, George. *This Way Miss*. unknown

Jessel, George, with John Austin. *The World I Lived In*. Chicago, Illinois: Henry Regnery Company. 1975

Jolson, Harry. with Alban Emley. *Mistah Jolson*. Hollywood, California: House-Warven. 1951

Kenrick, John. *A History of the Musical Minstrel Shows*.

Kobal, John. *Gotta Sing Gotta Dance-A Pictorial History of Film Musicals*, Middlesex, England: Hamlyn Publishing Group Limited. 1971

Laine, Frankie and Joseph Laredo. *That Lucky Old Son*. Ventura, California: Pathfinder Publishing. 1993

Martin, Mary. *My Heart Belongs*. New York, New York: William Morrow & Company. 1976.

Pleasants, Henry. *The Great American Popular Singers*. New York,

New York: Simon and Schuster. 1974

Rodgers, Richard. *Musical Stages*. New York, New York: Random House 1975

Shipp, Cameron. *Al Jolson, America's Minstrel Man*. New York, New York: Coronet Magazine-Esquire, Inc. Publishing. 1948

Theater Magazine- Editorial, October 1928. New York, New York. 1928

Thomas, Danny, *Make Room for Danny*. 1991

Velie, Lester. *Vocal Boy Makes Good*. New York, New York: Collier's Magazine. December 13, 1947

Whiting, Margaret and Will Holt. *It Might As Well Be Spring*. New York, New York: William Morrow & Company 1987.

Zolotow, Maurice. *Ageless Al*. Pleasantville, New York: Reader's Digest. January 1949

About The Author

Richard Grudens was initially influenced by Pulitzer Prize dramatist Robert Anderson; New York Herald Tribune columnist Will Cuppy; and detective/mystery novelist Dashiell Hammett, all whom he knew in his early years. Richard worked his way up from a studio page in NBC's studios in New York to news writer for various radio news programs and *The Bob and Ray Show* and TVs *Today Show.*

Feature writing for Long Island PM Magazine (1980-86) led to his first book, *The Best Damn Trumpet Player - Memories of the Big Band Era*. He has written over 100 magazine articles on diverse subjects from interviews with legendary cowboy Gene Autry in *Wild West Magazine* in 1995, to a treatise on the Beach Boys in the *California Highway Patrol Magazine*, and countless articles on Bing Crosby, Bob Hope, including a major Hope cover article covering Hope's famous wartime USO tours published in *World War II Magazine*. He has written about Henry Ford, VE Day, Motorcycle Helmet Safety and DNA History, among other subjects.

Other books include *The Song Stars* - 1997, *The Music Men* -1998, *Jukebox Saturday Night* - 1999, *Snootie Little Cutie - The Connie Haines Story* - 2000, *Jerry Vale - A Singer's Life* - 2001, *The Spirit of Bob Hope* - 2002, *Bing Crosby-Crooner of the Çentury* - 2003 (which won a Benjamin Franklin Award for Biography - Publishers Marketing Association), and *Chattanooga Choo Choo - The Life and Times of the World Famous Glenn Miller Orchestra* - 2004, and *The Italian Crooners Bedside Companion* in 2005.

Commenting about the book Jukebox Saturday Night in 1999, Kathryn (Mrs. Bing) Crosby wrote: "Richard Grudens is the musical historian of our time. Without him, the magic would be lost forever. We all owe him a debt that we can never repay."

Richard Grudens resides in St. James, New York.

Acknowledgments

You Ain't Read Nothin' Yet!

When a book is born, the many individuals, all friends and compatriots, who participated in its formation must be acknowledged for their contributions, however great or small, as no one can fully create a book alone:

Lots to be thankful for this 2006 Jolson Story.

Beginning with International Al Jolson Society President, Jan Hernstat, who helped pave the way for me, Journal Editor Stan Gerloff, intrepid Jolson scholar Ed Greenbaum, England's premier Jolson collector and scholar, Stan Ball of England, Jim Downs, Brian Decker and the list continues.

Thanks to my spirited gang of co-conspirators; my original mentor Frankie Laine, who penned a beautiful foreword; the magnificent Kathryn Crosby, who besides encouraging me, tells the world daily of the continuing legend of her husband Bing Crosby; Connie Haines, who knew and sang with Jolson and who still sings today, even over the telephone to me; Patty Andrews, who, with her sisters Maxine and La Verne, also sang and recorded with Jolson; Jolson co-star, the most gracious Sybil Jason and her diligent fan club president Gary Heckman; always there for me, the great Jerry Vale; Big Band Hall of Fame bandleader, my brother in music, Ben Grisafi; old friend Joe Franklin; Italian troubador Remo Capra, elite songwriter Ervin Drake; big band specialist and writer John Tumpak; writer and reviewer Jack Lebo; all around scribe and ultimate source detective Anthony Di Florio III; now a good friend, Jolson tribute performer Tony B. (Babino), Maria Babino (Tony's mom), son of great songwriter Gus Kahn, songwriter Donald Kahn; piano wizard John Primerano; my son Bob Grudens; friends, advisors and assistants Robert Incagliato, Jerry Castleman; radio personalities Max Wirz of Switzerland and Europe, legendary Jack Ellsworth of New York's WALK radio, and Al Monroe of New Jersey; and my wonderful wife, Madeline Grudens, who edits, formulates, provides photo magic, and shares in every aspect of the work.

And I will never forget a tribute to friends I shall miss, record collector and historian, Joe Pardee; eminent photographer and collaborator C. Camille Smith; friend and photographer Gus Young.

As Frankie Laine signs all his letters and photos, "May God Bless."

We are grateful to:

Madeline Grudens

Robert Grudens

Ben Grisafi

Bob Incagliato

Al Monroe

Max Wirz

Jack Ellsworth

Jerry Castleman

Jack Lebo

Additional Titles by Richard Grudens
www.RichardGrudens.com
Explore the Golden Age of Music when the Big Bands and their vocalists reigned on the radio and all the great stages of America.

The Italian Crooners Bedside Companion

The Italian Crooners is a compendium of your favorite Italian male singers, presented in a shower of photos, stories, favorite recipes and selected discographies with a foreword by Jerry Vale.

Chattanooga Choo Choo - The Life and Times of the World Famous Glenn Miller Orchestra

Commemorating the 100th Anniversary of Glenn Miller's life and the 60th Anniversary of his disappearance over the English Channel in late 1944, we present the tribute book Glenn Miller fans all over the world have been waiting for.

Bing Crosby - Crooner of the Century

Here is the quintessential Bing Crosby tribute, documenting the story of Crosby's colorful life, family, recordings, radio and television shows, and films; the amazing success story of a wondrous career that pioneered popular music spanning generations and inspiring countless followers.

The Spirit of Bob Hope:

Tracing Bob's charmed life from his early days in Cleveland to his worldwide fame earned in vaudeville, radio, television and films and his famous wartime travels for the USO unselfishly entertaining our troops. The best Bob Hope book with testimonials from his friends and a foreword by Jane Russell.

Jerry Vale - A Singer's Life

The wondrous story of Jerry's life as a kid from teeming Bronx streets of the 1940s to his legendary appearances in the great theatrical venues of America and his three triumphant Carnegie Hall concerts, with appearances at New York's Copacabana, whose magnificent voice has beautifully interpreted the 20th Century's most beautiful love songs

Snootie Little Cutie - The Connie Haines Story

The story of big band singer, Connie Haines, who sang shoulder to shoulder with Frank Sinatra in the bands of Harry James and Tommy Dorsey, and for years on the Abbott & Costello radio show, and who is still singing today.

Jukebox Saturday Night

The final book in the series; interviews with Artie Shaw, Les Brown and Doris Day, Red Norvo, Les Paul, Carmel Quinn, stories about Glenn Miller and the Dorsey Brothers, songwriters Ervin Drake ("I Believe," "It was a Very Good Year,") and Jack Lawrence ("Linda," "Tenderly,") and a special about all the European bands past and present.

Sally Bennett's Magic Moments

This book is filled with extraordinary events in the life of Sally Bennett who established the Big Band Hall of Fame and Museum in West Palm Beach, Florida. Sally is a composer, musician, playwright, model, actress, poet, radio and TV personality and the author of the book *Sugar and Spice*.

The Music Men

A Companion to "The Song Stars," about the great men singers with foreword by Bob Hope; interviews with Tony Martin, Don Cornell, Julius LaRosa, Jerry Vale, Joe Williams, Johnny Mathis, Al Martino, Guy Mitchell, Tex Beneke and others.

The Song Stars

A neat book about all the girl singers of the Big Band Era and beyond: Doris Day, Helen Forrest, Kitty Kallen, Rosemary Clooney, Jo Stafford, Connie Haines, Teresa Brewer, Patti Page and Helen O'Connell and many more.

The Best Damn Trumpet Player

Memories of the Big Band Era, interviews with Benny Goodman, Harry James, Woody Herman, Tony Bennett, Buddy Rich, Sarah Vaughan, Lionel Hampton, Frankie Laine, Patty Andrews and others.

Index

C

Caesar, Irving 48
Calloway, Cab 117, 234, 263
Cantor, Eddie 8, 25, 29, 59, 69, 112,
     117, 119, 121, 123, 170, 173,
     182, 251, 265
Cantor, Ida 119
Capote, Truman 191
Capra, Remo 269, 288
Carroll, Harry 68
Carson, Johnny 117, 124
Carter, Jack 124
Caruso, Enrico 120, 124, 185
Castleman, Jerry 288
Cavett, Dick 151
Chaplin, Charlie 80
Chaplin, Saul 241
Chaplin, Sydney 181
Chapman, Marguerite 180
Charles, Prince 273
Chevalier, Maurice 120
Clapton, Eric 272
Clark, Bobby 58
Clayton, Jackson & Durante 134
Clift, Montgomery 180
Clooney, Rosemary 196
Cohan, George M. 69, 79, 118, 120,
     185, 196, 215
Cohan, Jerry 79
Cohan, Josie 79
Cohan, Nellie 79
Cohn, Harry 136, 238
Cole, Natalie 272
Coleman, Cy 188
Coleman, Ronald 216
Como, Perry 90, 269
Conley, Anne-Marie 279
Conley, Brian Paul 273
Conn, Billy 126
Conrad, Con 211
Cooper, Pat 122
Coots, J. Fred 187
Cornell, Don 269
Cosby, Bill 151
Cosell, Howard 117, 124
Costello, Dolores 86

Costello, Lou 185
Crawford, Joan 71
Cristy, Edwin P. 45
Crosby, Bing 7, 15, 29, 52, 60, 88, 90,
     94, 95, 96, 97, 100, 105, 106,
     112, 120, 127, 141, 143, 189,
     196
Crosby, John 54
Crosby, Kathryn 9, 151, 288
Crosland, Alan 219

D

Damone, Vic 269
Darin, Bobby 52, 149, 270
Davis, Jr., Sammy 117, 122, 151
Day, Doris 149
Decker, Brian 152, 288
Delmar, Ethel 131
Demarest, William 243
DePippo, Angelo 261
Deslys, Gaby 39, 251
DeSylva, Buddy 48
Dillingham, Charles 250
Di Florio III, Anthony 30, 149, 288
Dockstader, Lew 25
Donaldson, Walter 211
Donath, Ludwig 243
Dorsey, Tommy 142, 270
Downs, Jim 111, 112, 288
Drake, Alfred 250
Drake, Anthony 159
Drake, Beatrice 85
Drake, Ervin 84, 288
Dressler, Marie 69
Drew, Ellen 180
Dubin, Al 191, 230, 231
Duke, Vernon 207
Dunn, Josephine 226
Durante, Jimmy 69, 117

E

Eckstine, Billy 165
Edison, Thomas 215
Einstein, Harry "Parkyakarcus" 96
Elgart, Larry 189
Ellen, Vera 196
Ellington, Duke 189